Nude with Violin

A Light Comedy in Three Acts

Noël Coward

A Samuel French Acting Edition

SAMUELFRENCH.COM
SAMUELFRENCH-LONDON.CO.UK

Copyright © 1956, 1958 by Noël Coward
Copyright © 1958 by (Revised Acting Edition) Noël Coward
All Rights Reserved

NUDE WITH VIOLIN is fully protected under the copyright laws of the United States of America, the British Commonwealth, including Canada, and all other countries of the Copyright Union. All rights, including professional and amateur stage productions, recitation, lecturing, public reading, motion picture, radio broadcasting, television and the rights of translation into foreign languages are strictly reserved.

ISBN 978-0-573-61318-0
www.SamuelFrench.com
www.SamuelFrench-London.co.uk

FOR PRODUCTION ENQUIRIES

UNITED STATES AND CANADA
Info@SamuelFrench.com
1-866-598-8449

UNITED KINGDOM AND EUROPE
Plays@SamuelFrench-London.co.uk
020-7255-4302

Each title is subject to availability from Samuel French, depending upon country of performance. Please be aware that *NUDE WITH VIOLIN* may not be licensed by Samuel French in your territory. Professional and amateur producers should contact the nearest Samuel French office or licensing partner to verify availability.

CAUTION: Professional and amateur producers are hereby warned that *NUDE WITH VIOLIN* is subject to a licensing fee. Publication of this play(s) does not imply availability for performance. Both amateurs and professionals considering a production are strongly advised to apply to Samuel French before starting rehearsals, advertising, or booking a theatre. A licensing fee must be paid whether the title(s) is presented for charity or gain and whether or not admission is charged. Professional/Stock licensing fees are quoted upon application to Samuel French.

No one shall make any changes in this title(s) for the purpose of production. No part of this book may be reproduced, stored in a retrieval system, or transmitted in any form, by any means, now known or yet to be invented, including mechanical, electronic, photocopying, recording, videotaping, or otherwise, without the prior written permission of the publisher. No one shall upload this title(s), or part of this title(s), to any social media websites.

For all enquiries regarding motion picture, television, and other media rights, please contact Samuel French.

Please refer to page 94 for further copyright information.

NUDE WITH VIOLIN

STORY OF THE PLAY

Here is the latest confection from the pen of one of the most versatile writers of this era: witty, entertaining—and unmistakably Noël Coward. As it must to lesser men, death came even to the brilliant painter, Paul Sorodin. And indecently close to death's heels came Sorodin's bereaved relatives, his business manager, and all those others who, their grief not entirely untinged with greed, anxiously awaited the reading of the great man's will. It was the propitious moment for Sébastien, valet and companion extraordinary to Sorodin, to step in with some jolting surprises for the assembled "mourners." One of the jolts was a letter he produced making it clear that Paul Sorodin was not all he had seemed—which is a fine and merry way to start off a Coward play. Also on hand with a few revelations of their own were: an eccentric Russian Princess, an ex-show girl, an Eleventh Hour Immersionist (a very avant-garde religion), and a mute but effective gentleman named Fabrice. Before they got through, reputations were arranged and rearranged, Sébastien emerged with a tidy little nest egg for his old age —and delighted audiences both in London and New York had the time of their lives. *The smartest comedy of the season . . . bright and brittle humor, loads of laughs . . . "Nude With Violin" spells hilarity as slick as a seal's overcoat. Robert Coleman in the New York Daily Mirror.*

NUDE WITH VIOLIN, produced in America at the Belasco Theatre, 44th Street, New York, on November 14, 1957. It was presented by The Playwrights' Company and Lance Hamilton and Charles Russell, with the following cast:

SEBASTIEN .... *Noël Coward*
MARIE-CELESTE .... *Therese Quadri*
CLINTON PREMINGER, JUNIOR.. *William Taylor*
ISOBEL SORODIN............... *Joyce Carey*
JANE .... *Angela Thornton*
COLIN .... *John Ainsworth*
PAMELA .... *Iola Lynn*
JACOB FRIEDLAND .... *Morris Carnovsky*
ANYA PAVLIKOV............... *Luba Malina*
CHERRY-MAY WATERTON ... *Mona Washbourne*
FABRICE .... *Robert Thurston*
OBADIAH LEWELLYN .... *Cory Devlin*
GEORGE .... *Robert Wark*
STOTESBURY .... *Bobby Alford*

The play directed by
Noël Coward

with setting by
Oliver Smith

SCENES

The action of the play takes place in Paul Sorodin's Studio in Paris

TIME
The Present.

ACT ONE
Afternoon.

ACT TWO
Scene 1
A few hours later.

Scene 2
The following afternoon.

ACT THREE
Scene 1
A few hours later.

Scene 2
The following morning.

Nude with Violin

ACT ONE

SETTING: *The scene is* PAUL SORODIN'S *studio in Paris. It is large and luxuriously furnished. There are some fine paintings and sculptures but no evidence of* SORODIN'S *own work. In the Center there are two double doors which open into a hall and thence to the front door. Down Right a small door leads to the library. Above this is a solid writing-desk. The Left wall is taken up by a vast window through which can be seen trees and the roofs of houses in the distance. A couple of modern armchairs and a sofa are placed at the director's discretion. There is a refectory table under the window set with cakes and sandwiches and a magnum of champagne ornamented with a large black bow.*

AT RISE: *When the CURTAIN rises it is about four o'clock on a summer afternoon in the year 1954. After a moment or two,* SEBASTIEN LACRÉOLE *enters, bearing two plates of patisserie. He is a dark, rather swarthy man and might be any age between forty and fifty-five. He is impeccably dressed in black trousers and a white coat, on the left sleeve of which there is a wide mourning band of black silk. As he puts the plates on the table the TELEPHONE rings. He goes to it.*

SEBASTIEN. (*At telephone.*) Allô—J'écoute—ici Invalides 2645—Oui, monsieur—Non, monsieur—Oui, monsieur, je suis complètement d'accord: pour nous c'est une tragédie mais pour le monde, une catastrophe. Merci, monsieur—Monsieur est trop aimable—Sans faute, monsieur—Au revoir, monsieur. (*He hangs up the receiver and is about to return to the table when the FRONT DOOR BELL rings. He crosses and opens the drapes.* MARIE-CELESTE, *a middle-aged "Bonne," enters.*)

MARIE-CELESTE. Il y a un monsieur à la porte.

SEBASTIEN. Quelle espèce de monsieur?

MARIE-CELESTE. Je ne sais pas, je ne suis pas clairvoyante moi, je crois qu'il est Anglais ou peut-être Américain.

SEBASTIEN. Journaliste?

MARIE-CELESTE. Écoutes, mon coco, comment est ce-que je peux te dire? Je lui ai dit rien que Bon Jour.

SEBASTIEN. Merde!

MARIE-CELESTE. D'accord. Je m'en fou de tout ce bruit.

CLINTON. (*At this moment* CLINTON PREMINGER, *junior, comes tentatively into the room. He is an earnest-looking young American in the late twenties or early thirties. Laboriously.*) Excusez-moi.

SEBASTIEN. Monsieur?

CLINTON. Parlez-vous anglais?

SEBASTIEN. Yes, monsieur.

CLINTON. Thank God. (MARIE-CELESTE *exits.*)

SEBASTIEN. This is a house of mourning, monsieur.

CLINTON. I know. That's why I'm here—I mean I have to see Madame Sorodin, it's business—urgent business.

SEBASTIEN. Madame Sorodin has not yet returned from the funeral and when she does I feel that she will be in no mood to discuss business, however urgent.

CLINTON. I guess you're Sébastien.

SEBASTIEN. Your guess is correct, monsieur.

CLINTON. I have some notes on you.

SEBASTIEN. Have you indeed?

CLINTON. I represent *Life* Magazine.

SEBASTIEN. It is in questionable taste to force *Life* Magazine into a house of death, monsieur.

CLINTON. My name is Clinton Preminger, junior.

SEBASTIEN. It would be all the same if you were Clinton Preminger, senior.

CLINTON. Now see here, I'm not an ordinary press reporter out for scoop headlines, I'm a serious writer.
SEBASTIEN. I am delighted to hear it.
CLINTON. For over two years I've been assembling material for a comprehensive study of Sorodin and his paintings. It's to be called "Triton among the Minnows."
SEBASTIEN. Most appropriate.
CLINTON. I came by sea to give myself time to get all my notes in order and when I landed at Cherbourg I found that he had died. You can imagine the shock!
SEBASTIEN. It was a shock to the whole world, monsieur.
MARIE-CELESTE. (*Entering from service door with a jar of pâté.*) Il est beau gars, qu'est-ce qu'il dit?
SEBASTIEN. (*Crossing to* MARIE-CELESTE *and taking the pâté.*) Rien d'importance . . . sauve toi!
MARIE-CELESTE. Bon. Je me sauve. (*She goes out.*)
SEBASTIEN. You say you have some notes on me? What sort of notes?
CLINTON. Merely factual. I have them here in my file —just a moment. (*Looks in file.*) S. S. Sébastien.
SEBASTIEN. I sound like an Atlantic liner.
CLINTON. Sébastien Lacreeole. Is that right?
SEBASTIEN. Not quite. There should be an accent on the first E in Lacréole.
CLINTON. My French isn't too good.
SEBASTIEN. You must persevere.
CLINTON. (*Consulting his notes.*) You entered the service of Paul Sorodin in July 1946 in the capacity of valet.
SEBASTIEN. Correct.
CLINTON. You don't talk like a valet.
SEBASTIEN. You can't have everything.
CLINTON. You are of mixed parentage.
SEBASTIEN. You have a genius for understatement, monsieur.
CLINTON. Born in Martinique, date uncertain.
SEBASTIEN. My whole life has been uncertain.
CLINTON. (*Still at his notes.*) Deported from Syria in 1929. No offence specified.

SEBASTIEN. The Syrians are terribly vague.

CLINTON. Imprisoned in Saigon 1933. Offence specified.

SEBASTIEN. (*Reminiscently.*) I remember it well.

CLINTON. Resident in England 1936.

SEBASTIEN. The happiest time of my life.

CLINTON. Landed in Los Angeles 1937.

SEBASTIEN. The saddest.

CLINTON. Married in Rio de Janeiro 1939. Wife living.

SEBASTIEN. With a customs officer.

CLINTON. From 1942 to 1946, proprietor of a rooming-house in Mexico City.

SEBASTIEN. Your delicacy does you credit, monsieur.

CLINTON. (*Closing file.*) Those are all my notes on you up to date.

SEBASTIEN. Quite accurate as far as they go.

CLINTON. (*Earnestly.*) I'd like you to understand that by reading them to you I had no intention of embarrassing you.

SEBASTIEN. Thank you. You didn't.

CLINTON. I despise moral attitudes. I believe that life is for living, don't you?

SEBASTIEN. It's difficult to know what else one could do with it.

CLINTON. Personally I have no inhibitions. I took a course of psychiatry at Yale.

SEBASTIEN. That explains everything.

CLINTON. I've studied Jung and Freud and Adler and Kinsey and all the big boys.

SEBASTIEN. Mr. Kinsey himself studied quite a number of the big boys.

CLINTON. What I mean to say is that nothing shocks me. I think that every man should do what he wants to do.

SEBASTIEN. A tolerant philosophy but apt to lead to untidiness.

CLINTON. Where did you learn to speak such good English?

SEBASTIEN. The Esplanade Hotel, Bournemouth.

CLINTON. What were you doing there?

SEBASTIEN. Looking after an elderly lady. No offence specified.

CLINTON. You liked working for Paul Sorodin?

SEBASTIEN. Very much indeed, monsieur. He was a great man.

CLINTON. Was he difficult, temperamental? I mean did he fly into violent rages?

SEBASTIEN. Frequently.

CLINTON. Did he ever strike you?

SEBASTIEN. No. He once threw a pork chop at me but it only broke the clock.

CLINTON. (*Scribbling a note.*) Excuse me.

SEBASTIEN. I really think, Monsieur Preminger, that as Madame Sorodin may return from Père-Lachaise at any moment, it would be tactful of you to leave now. The presence here of a stranger would be an intrusion on her grief.

CLINTON. Grief? Just a moment— (*He searches through his file, finds a paper and scans it.*) Sorodin deserted her in 1926, didn't he?

SEBASTIEN. 1925.

CLINTON. And she hasn't seen him since?

SEBASTIEN. I believe that they once met by accident in the Galeries Lafayette.

CLINTON. I shouldn't imagine she'd be suffering much grief after all those years.

SEBASTIEN. (*Reprovingly.*) He was her husband and the father of her children.

CLINTON. Why did she never divorce him?

SEBASTIEN. She is a woman of the highest principles, and a Catholic.

CLINTON. Can you beat that?

SEBASTIEN. People have tried, monsieur, but seldom with unqualified success.

CLINTON. Tell me. Did he hate her?

SEBASTIEN. Not at all. He once painted a moustache on her photograph but only in a spirit of fun.

CLINTON. (*Rising.*) You know, I like you, Sébastien.

SEBASTIEN. Thank you.

CLINTON. I really am crazy to meet Madame Sorodin. Can I stay until she arrives if I promise to go the moment you tip me the wink?

SEBASTIEN. It would be as much as my place is worth.

CLINTON. But your place can't be worth much now anyway, can it?

SEBASTIEN. That remains to be seen.

CLINTON. Are you taken care of in the will?

SEBASTIEN. Mr. Sorodin left no will.

CLINTON. Gosh! That means that everything will go to her, doesn't it?

SEBASTIEN. I presume so.

CLINTON. No wonder she came haring over here for the public funeral.

SEBASTIEN. Your flippancy appals me, monsieur.

CLINTON. Do you like her?

SEBASTIEN. I am in no position to say, having only just met her.

CLINTON. Does she like you?

SEBASTIEN. I doubt it, monsieur. Paul Sorodin was more than my employer, he was my friend. I travelled with him far and wide. He found me good company: we laughed together and drank together and took our pleasures lightly. Whether Madame Sorodin liked me or not I am fairly sure that she could never approve of me. Our views of life are so diametrically opposed.

CLINTON. I'll bet the hell they are.

(*The TELEPHONE rings.*)

SEBASTIEN. Excuse me. (*He goes to telephone.*) Allô j'écoute—ici Invalides 2645—Si Señor—Aun no, Señor —Si Señor, estamos completamente de acuerdo, para nosotros es una tragedia, pero para el mundo es una catástrofe—Muchas gracias Señor—Usted es muy amable Señor—Sin falta Señor—Hasta luego Señor. (*He hangs up.*)

CLINTON. How many languages do you speak?

SEBASTIEN. Fourteen, including dialects. My Swahili

is a bit rusty at the moment; there are so few opportunities of speaking it in Paris.

CLINTON. Was Sorodin a linguist?

SEBASTIEN. Only when he was drunk.

CLINTON. Was he a heavy drinker?

SEBASTIEN. In certain circumstances, yes, but sometimes he would go for hours without touching a drop.

CLINTON. Are you laughing at me by any chance?

SEBASTIEN. A little, Monsieur Preminger.

CLINTON. Why? What is there about me that's so funny?

SEBASTIEN. Your naïveté, monsieur. If, as you say, you intend to write a serious biography of Paul Sorodin I cannot help feeling that your approach should be a trifle less ingenuous.

CLINTON. My approach is logical. Facts first, analysis afterwards. You must know more about him than anybody. You could help me a lot if only you would.

SEBASTIEN. Why should I?

CLINTON. For the sake of posterity, if for no other reason.

SEBASTIEN. Sorodin will be remembered even without the aid of *Life* Magazine, Monsieur Preminger, and within a few years your biography of him will only be one among hundreds. (*The FRONT DOOR BELL rings.*) Here they are. You'd better go.

CLINTON. Five minutes, just five minutes—you promised.

SEBASTIEN. I did no such thing.

CLINTON. Please. I swear I'll go the moment you give me the hint.

SEBASTIEN. What sort of hint can I possibly give you?

CLINTON. Offer me a cigarette. I shall refuse it and leave at once.

SEBASTIEN. (*Weakening.*) It is all highly irregular.

CLINTON. Please. Be a pal. It means so much to me. And call me at the hotel later and we can make a date for dinner.

SEBASTIEN. Which hotel?

CLINTON. The George V.
SEBASTIEN. I might have known it.
CLINTON. Okay?
SEBASTIEN. (*Resigned.*) Okay.

(MARIE-CELESTE *flings open the double doors and stands aside to allow* ISOBEL, JANE, COLIN, PAMELA *and* JACOB FRIEDLAND *to enter. They are all, naturally, in mourning.* ISOBEL, *a woman in the early fifties, is a fairly typical example of the English upper middle-class. Her clothes are well cut but in no way remarkable. At the moment she looks a trifle harassed. She sits in the armchair.* COLIN, *her son, although not in uniform, is quite unmistakably a major in the Army; he stands behind* ISOBEL. PAMELA, *his wife, is equally unmistakably the wife of a major in the Army. She has a forthright manner and is accustomed to speaking her mind which limits the scope of her conversation.* JANE *differs from her mother and brother in that she has a definite style of her own and a sense of humour which perhaps she has inherited from her father.* JACOB FRIEDLAND, *an art dealer of considerable renown, is dapper, shrewd and kindly enough although his manner is inclined to be pompous and didactic on occasion.*)

ISOBEL. (*As she comes in.*) It was all very impressive and really very moving but I am thankful that it is over.

MARIE-CELESTE. Madame a besoin de quelque chose? Un cachet Faivre peut-être?

ISOBEL. No—non merci beaucoup. (MARIE-CELESTE *retires.*)

JACOB. (*Seeing* CLINTON. *To* SEBASTIEN.) Who is this?

SEBASTIEN. Monsieur Clinton Preminger, junior, monsieur. He represents *Life* Magazine.

JACOB. I thought my instructions were quite clear, Sébastien.

CLINTON. Please don't blame him, sir, it's all my fault. He tried to make me go but I wouldn't.

JACOB. I am afraid I must ask you to leave immediately. This is a moment when privacy should be respected.

CLINTON. Are you Mr. Jacob Friedland?

JACOB. I am.

CLINTON. I have some notes on you.

JACOB. Kindly show Mr. Preminger out, Sébastien.

CLINTON. Just a moment, please. Mrs. Sorodin, I appeal to you. I am writing a series of articles on your late husband's work. I know that you have lived apart from him for many years but you must still feel in your heart a little tenderness for him, you who once held him in your arms—

SEBASTIEN. A cigarette, Monsieur Preminger?

CLINTON. (*Absently taking one.*) Thanks.

JACOB. Mr. Preminger—

CLINTON. And you, Mr. Friedland. You who braved the ignorant scorn of his early critics and set his feet so firmly on the ladder of success.

SEBASTIEN. (*With an edge to his voice.*) A light, Monsieur Preminger? For your cigarette!

CLINTON. (*Automatically.*) Thanks. (SEBASTIEN *shrugs his shoulders and lights his cigarette.*) Please help me, Mr. Friedland, in the same spirit that you have helped and encouraged talent all your life—Mrs. Sorodin, I appeal to you again—

ISOBEL. (*Flustered.*) Oh dear—this is really most awkward—I don't know what to say—Jane—Colin—

COLIN. I'll deal with this. (*To* CLINTON.) Now look here, young man. I don't care what magazine you represent or who you are or where you come from, but if you don't leave this house within fifty seconds I'll throw you out.

JACOB. Just a moment, Colin. (*To* CLINTON.) I fully appreciate your position, Mr. Preminger, and I will do all I can to help you on condition that you leave us alone now in the private sorrow that has come to us.

CLINTON. (*Carried away.*) It's not a private sorrow, it's a public disaster!

SEBASTIEN. (*Menacingly.*) Another cigarette, Monsieur Preminger?

COLIN. What the devil do you keep offering him cigarettes for?

CLINTON. (*Stricken.*) Cigarette!—My God!—Sorry, Sébastien. Good-bye. (*He goes rapidly out of the room.*)

PAMELA. (*After a slight pause.*) The man's obviously a lunatic.

SEBASTIEN. No, madame, merely an enthusiast. He took a course of psychiatry at Yale.

PAMELA. What's Yale?

ISOBEL. It's a university in America, dear, just like Cambridge you know only quite different.

COLIN. He'd have been better advised to take a course in manners.

JACOB. You had no business to let him in, Sébastien. I am very displeased.

COLIN. I suppose he bribed you.

JANE. (*Frowning.*) Really, Colin.

SEBASTIEN. I am not in the habit of accepting bribes, sir.

JANE. I'm sure you're not, Sébastien.

SEBASTIEN. Thank you, miss.

JANE. Where did you learn to speak such perfect English?

SEBASTIEN. In Bournemouth, miss. I was in service there some years ago.

PAMELA. Domestic service?

SEBASTIEN. Some of my duties were almost overwhelmingly domestic. May I offer Mesdames, Messieurs some refreshment?

JANE. I must say I should love a drink, it's been a very tiring day.

SEBASTIEN. (*Picks up magnum of champagne from bar table.*) Champagne, miss?

JANE. Yes please, that would be lovely.

COLIN. Good Lord! A Magnum! Where did that come from?

SEBASTIEN. It was a Christmas present from Mr. Sorodin. I wished to contribute in my own humble way to this melancholy but historic occasion. (*To* ISOBEL.) I hope Madame will accept it in the spirit in which it is offered?

ISOBEL. Really—I hardly know what to say—thank you, Sébastien—hand me my bag, Pamela dear, if I am going to have champagne I must take off my hat.

SEBASTIEN. (*Opens bottle and fills glasses.*) I would like to repudiate the black bow. It was Marie-Céleste's idea. She has an exaggerated sense of *fantaisie*. (ISOBEL *takes off her hat and pats her hair into place with the aid of her hand mirror.*)

JANE. (*Handing* ISOBEL *a glass of wine.*) Here, mother, it will do you good. (*The champagne is handed round.*)

ISOBEL. I doubt that, Jane. Champagne really doesn't agree with me, the last time I had any was at poor Ettie's wedding—you remember, Colin—I was ill for days.

JACOB. Perhaps it was a bad year.

ISOBEL. Oh indeed it was, everything went wrong.

JANE. You must drink, too, Sébastien.

SEBASTIEN. Thank you, miss, I will be honoured.

JACOB. By all means. Fill a glass for him, Colin. (COLIN *fills a wine glass.*)

SEBASTIEN. May I be permitted to propose a toast?

COLIN. Oh God! (*Handing glass to* SEBASTIEN.)

JANE. Shut up, Colin. Please do, Sébastien.

SEBASTIEN. (*Raising his glass.*) I drink to the memory of my master Paul Sorodin. A man of charm and humour and courage: a man who, until death smudged out the twinkle in his eye, contrived to enjoy life to the full and at the same time remain a hero to his own valet. Madame. Ladies and Gentlemen. Paul Sorodin. (*He drains his glass in one gulp, dashes it to the floor and goes swiftly out of the room.*)

PAMELA. (*After a slight pause.*) Well really—what a funny thing to do!

ISOBEL. A little theatrical perhaps, dear, but after all he *is* a foreigner.

PAMELA. I can't stand him, it's no use I just can't stand him. He gives me the creeps.

JANE. I rather like him.

PAMELA. Really, Jane, what is there about him that you could possibly like?

JANE. He has charm, I think.

COLIN. (*Contemptuously.*) Charm! The chap's a Dago. I wouldn't trust him an inch.

PAMELA. A strong touch of the tar brush, if you ask me.

JANE. Nobody did, Pamela.

PAMELA. There is no need to be rude.

JANE. Father was obviously devoted to him.

COLIN. He looks a thoroughly sinister type to me.

JANE. We have no proof that Sébastian is a sinister type. We met him for the first time two days ago.

COLIN. You have only to look at him. I know the sort. Oily.

JANE. I liked what he said about father.

ISOBEL. I know that over the years you have built up in your mind a romantic conception of your father, Jane darling—

JANE. He was a romantic man.

ISOBEL. I also know, modern values being what they are, that you can see nothing wrong in the unprincipled life he chose to lead.

JANE. Men of genius see life in their own terms; their principles are different from those of ordinary people.

ISOBEL. I am sure I have no wish to argue with you, but I do think you might spare a little of your loyalty to your poor mother, rather than devote it all to the man who betrayed her and made her life a hell upon earth.

COLIN. Hear, hear.

JANE. (*Smiling.*) Darling mother, what absolute nonsense! You lived with father for exactly six years. Admittedly your life may have been a bit difficult for that very brief period, but since then it has been extremely comfortable.

ISOBEL. I have no intention of pursuing this discussion

any further, Jane, it is really most unsuitable considering why we are here and everything.

JANE. Did you love my father, Jacob?

JACOB. His impact on my world, the world of Art, was stupendous; his influence far reaching and incalculable.

JANE. But you were fond of him—as a man I mean? Did you look forward to seeing him, to dining with him? Was he gay and attractive and good company?

JACOB. He could be all those things when he chose.

PAMELA. But his paintings! I know I'm ignorant and don't know anything about art really, but what do they *mean?* I've never been able to understand.

JACOB. (*Portentously.*) Go into the Tate Gallery, my dear, and look at Sorodin's "Portrait of Marjorie." Stand before it quietly, receptively. Stand for an hour, two hours, three hours if need be, then go away.

PAMELA. Three hours is an awfully long time.

JACOB. It takes a lifetime to appreciate a masterpiece.

COLIN. Is "Portrait of Marjorie" the one with all those rings and dots?

JACOB. It is the apotheosis of his "Circular" period. One of the few great modern paintings in the world.

COLIN. But why is it called "Portrait of Marjorie"? It isn't a portrait at all. I mean it isn't like anyone or anything.

JACOB. (*Patiently.*) It is Sorodin's abstract conception of a woman called Marjorie.

PAMELA. Marjorie who?

JANE. Does it matter?

JACOB. (*Giving up.*) The fact remains that the Tate bought "Portrait of Marjorie" for three thousand pounds in 1936. It would be worth treble the amount today.

COLIN. Well, it's beyond me, that's all I can say, I can't make head or tail of it.

JACOB. Sorodin's creative genius was concentrated into three great periods. The first, what is now described as his "Farouche" period, lasted from 1927 until the early thirties. His first exhibition caused an uproar. There were jeers and catcalls. One elderly art critic struck at one of the canvases with his umbrella. A lady from Des Moines, Iowa, fainted dead away and had to be taken to the American hospital.

ISOBEL. Poor thing. That's where they took poor Edith Carrington when she had that dreadful rash.

JACOB. The "Circular" period was an evolution and a reaction at the same time. Through the dark years of the war I had no message from him. Indeed I imagined he must be dead. It was not until he returned to Paris in 1946 that I realised the full significance of the private war he had been waging with his own genius, a struggle that resulted in the greatest victory of his career. The "Jamaican" period.

COLIN. All those fat negresses?

JACOB. (*Sharply.*) Yes, all those fat negresses, all that primitive simplicity and glorious colour as well. The first painting he showed me on that fabulous day is now in the Louvre.

JANE. "Girl with Breadfruit"?

JACOB. No. "Boy with Plantain." "Girl with Breadfruit" is in Prague.

ISOBEL. That was the one we used for our Christmas cards the year before last, you remember, Colin? Your Aunt Freda wrote "Indecent" on it in red ink and sent it back.

SEBASTIEN. (*Enters.*) You rang, madame?

JACOB. No, Sébastien. Nobody rang.

SEBASTIEN. How curious! I was certain I heard a bell. Perhaps it was a bicycle. Have you everything you want?

JACOB. Yes, thank you.

SEBASTIEN. Perhaps Madame would care for a little caviar?

ISOBEL. No thank you, Sébastien.

SEBASTIEN. We still have several tins left over. Professor Vladimir Kashkov used to have it flown to us regularly from Moscow in the diplomatic pouch. He was an ardent admirer of Mr. Sorodin.

COLIN. Diplomatic pouch?

SEBASTIEN. (*With a smile.*) Yes. He was a spy in the American Embassy, until he was transferred.

COLIN. You mean that my father was in the habit of accepting presents from a Communist traitor?

SEBASTIEN. Your father was in the habit of accepting presents from anyone who chose to give them to him, sir. Right up to the last he used to look forward to his birthday with the enthusiastic exuberance of a small boy. It was one of his most endearing characteristics.

COLIN. Endearing characteristics my foot. He ought to have been ashamed of himself.

SEBASTIEN. (*Reprovingly.*) That would never have occurred to him, sir, in any circumstances whatsoever.

JANE. Do try not to be so overbearingly truculent, Colin.

SEBASTIEN. Mr. Sorodin was temperamentally incapable of political prejudice. Also, he was devoted to caviar.

ISOBEL. Personally I can never understand what people see in it. It's so fishy.

SEBASTIEN. (*Charmingly.*) Almost everything that comes from Russia nowadays is liable to be a bit fishy, madame.

JACOB. You say this Professor what's-his-name was transferred. Where was he transferred to?

SEBASTIEN. He is at present serving on a security commission in Washington, sir. (*Goes out.*)

COLIN. Well I'll be damned!

ISOBEL. Hush, Colin. I'm afraid your poor father was always attracted to disreputable characters. Do you remember, Jacob, that dreadful Rumanian with a guitar? He stayed in the house for weeks until I put my foot down.

JANE. (*Laughing.*) More champagne, mother?

ISOBEL. No thank you, dear.

JANE. (*Rising.*) I'd like some more and I'm sure Jacob would. He's had a horrid week dealing with everything. (*She goes to the table.*)

ISOBEL. You've been most considerate, Jacob, to make all the arrangements and support me through today's ordeal. I could never have endured it without you.

JANE. You really shouldn't have come, mother.

ISOBEL. Nonsense, dear, it was my duty.

JANE. Personally I think it was unnecessary. Nobody was deceived.

ISOBEL. What a disagreeable thing to say, Jane. I'm sure I had no wish to deceive anyone.

COLIN. Jane's been in a bad mood all day, argumentative and thoroughly tiresome. (*To* JANE.) Why don't you snap out of it?

JANE. I haven't been anything of the sort, but I hated us being here, I hated the whole business, all those crowds and press cameras and professional mourners. I felt ashamed.

JACOB. It was most important from every point of view for Paul Sorodin's widow and children to be present at his funeral.

JANE. Every point of view but father's.

ISOBEL. Really, **Jane**.

JANE. He'd have **thought** we were hypocrites, as indeed we were.

ISOBEL. I resent your attitude, Jane. Your father was my husband—

JANE. He wouldn't have been if only you had divorced him when he wanted you to, years ago.

PAMELA. I must say this is hardly the moment to go into all that.

ISOBEL. Pamela is quite right. This is indeed no moment to go into that. You should be ashamed of yourself.

JANE. I am, I've already said so, I'm ashamed of us all. Allowing ourselves to be photographed all ends up looking like a lot of black crows.

COLIN. Why don't you stop upsetting mother? She has enough to put up with, God knows.

JANE. She has nothing whatever to put up with. I don't blame her for hating father, we all know he behaved badly to her in the past and deserted her and made her miserable, but all that was years and years ago.

COLIN. What's the point of raking it all up now, then?

JANE. What I do blame her for is not setting him free when he wanted to be set free and on top of that making us all come traipsing over here to cash in on his death.

ISOBEL. Once and for all, Jane, I forbid you to talk like that. You are perfectly well aware that even if I had been willing to divorce your father, to have done so would directly have contravened the canons of my Faith. I know you have grown apart from us during the last few years, I expect it is my fault, everything is always my fault. But I must say I have been deeply grieved by your attitude to me throughout all this trying ordeal. I feel utterly exhausted. Colin, will you and Pamela take me back to the hotel. I have no more to say.

JANE. I'm sorry, mother. I didn't mean to grieve you, but I do wish you could see my point just a little.

ISOBEL. You should never have taken that Journalism course at the Polytechnic, it's ruined your character.

JANE. Oh, mother, you are funny, really you are.

ISOBEL. I'm sure I don't see anything to laugh at.

JANE. Are you really cross or only pretending to be?

ISOBEL. I don't know what you mean.

JANE. Well, you've been pretending to be sad all day, I see no reason why you shouldn't be pretending to be upset now.

ISOBEL. (*Rising.*) Come, Colin. (COLIN *rises.*)

JANE. (*Sitting* ISOBEL *down again.*) You can't possibly go away before we've decided what's to be done about Sébastien.

COLIN. Sébastien? What are you talking about? Why should anything be done about him?

JANE. Father left no will. Sébastien served him faithfully during his last years. Something will have to be done about him.

PAMELA. I expect he has taken good care to feather his own nest.

JANE. Jacob. Do you agree with me?

JACOB. There is certainly something in what you say.

COLIN. Pay him a month's wages and good riddance.

JANE. That's not enough. We're leaving first thing in the morning. It must be settled before we go.

PAMELA. I agree with Colin. Give him a month's wages and send him away with a flea in his ear.

JANE. He must have a pension.

COLIN. Pension! You must be out of your mind.

JANE. It's a question of common decency. Mother, you as father's widow cannot afford to appear mean in the eyes of the world. You can't repay his years of devotion to father with a month's wages. What do you think, Jacob?

JACOB. In the circumstances I think Jane is right.

COLIN. Well, I'm damned if I do.

PAMELA. Neither do I.

ISOBEL. Is that your considered opinion, Jacob?

JACOB. Yes. I think he should be given the choice of a pension or a lump sum, whichever he prefers.

ISOBEL. Oh dear. Well, if you really feel it's necessary, I suppose we must agree. Will you interview him?

JACOB. Willingly. But I think it would be more tactful if you told him yourself.

ISOBEL. I have already told you I'm tired, Jacob. I want to go back to the hotel and lie down.

JACOB. He is a very articulate man, Isobel. There is nothing to prevent him giving all sorts of interviews to the Press. A gesture from you at this particular moment would, I am sure, be a wise move.

ISOBEL. (*Resigned.*) Very well. Ring for him.

COLIN. (*Presses the bell near the service door.*) Bear up, mother. We can always rely on you to say the right thing.

ISOBEL. Thank you, dear.

SEBASTIEN. (*Comes into the room. He is wearing an expression of polite subservience.*) You rang, madame?

ISOBEL. (*In command.*) Yes, Sébastien. I wish to speak to you for a moment.

SEBASTIEN. At your service, madame.

ISOBEL. First of all I want to thank you for the—er—loyal service you gave my late husband. I would like to say that I find your obvious devotion to him touching, really most touching.

SEBASTIEN. Thank you, madame.

ISOBEL. As you are no doubt aware, Mr. Sorodin left no will.

SEBASTIEN. Yes, madame. I am aware of that.

ISOBEL. And—er—realising that his sudden death might have left you in an embarrassing situation—

SEBASTIEN. In what way, madame?

ISOBEL. (*With an effort.*) Financially.

SEBASTIEN. The financial aspect has not yet occurred to me. Doubtless it will later.

ISOBEL. (*Flummoxed*). Oh.

SEBASTIEN. I have frequently been embarrassed in my life, madame, but more often by lack of taste than by lack of money. (*The TELEPHONE rings.*) Excuse me. (*He goes to it and lifts the receiver.*) Allô: J'écoute—ici Invalides 2645—Ja, mein Herr—Nein, mein Herr—Ja, ich bin vollkommen Ihrer Meinung—für uns ist es eine Tragödie, für die Welt, aber, ist es eine Katastrophe—Ja, mein Herr—Ich danke Ihnen. (*He laughs heartily.*) Auf Wiedersehen, mein Herr. (*He hangs up.*)

JACOB. What was all that about?

SEBASTIEN. Merely a message of condolence, sir. That was Herr Otto Grunschnabel, the director of the "Health in Art" Centre in Hamburg. It is a really remarkable organisation. All art students of both sexes between the ages of fifteen and twenty-five are taken in groups into the fields twice a week to establish contact with natural phenomena and acquire physical fitness at the same time.

JANE. I didn't know there were any fields in Hamburg.

SEBASTIEN. There aren't. They go by electric train and trudge back in formation, dragging their easels. Herr Grunschnabel was a great friend of Mr. Sorodin's. When we were in Germany he used to supply us with models.

COLIN. (*Contemptuously.*) Models!

SEBASTIEN. A comprehensive term, sir. (*To* ISOBEL.) You were about to say, madame?—

ISOBEL. I was about to say that, in consideration of your services to my late husband, Mr. Friedland and I have decided to offer you the choice of a sum of money to be paid in the near future, or—or a small pension. Which would you prefer?

SEBASTIEN. Without wishing to be discourteous, neither, madame.

PAMELA. Well, really!

SEBASTIEN. Please believe me when I say how profoundly I appreciate your kindness and consideration. To you, Miss Jane, and you, Mr. Friedland, I must also express my gratitude. I happened to be listening outside the door just now when the matter was being discussed.

COLIN. Typical! Exactly what I should have expected.

JANE. (*Amused.*) That was disgraceful of you, Sébastien.

SEBASTIEN. You will understand therefore how much it pains me, in the face of such spontaneous generosity— to be the bearer of what I fear will be most disturbing news.

JACOB. Disturbing news! What do you mean?

SEBASTIEN. "Ah what a dusty answer gets the soul when hot for certainties in this our life."

COLIN. What on earth are you talking about?

SEBASTIEN. That was Mr. George Meredith's rather involved way of saying, sir, "The best laid schemes O' mice and men gang aft agley." Although Mr. Sorodin left no will, he *did* leave a letter.

JACOB. Letter?

SEBASTIEN. A personal letter addressed to me. It was written in the early hours of the morning of January the First of this year and was witnessed by Marie-Céleste and the head waiter from the "Grâce à Dieu." He had organized the catering.

COLIN. Catering?

SEBASTIEN. We had given a little party. Nothing grandiose you understand, just a small gathering of intimate

ACT I   NUDE WITH VIOLIN   27

friends, quite informal. In fact it was so informal one of the guests—

JACOB. (*Obviously disturbed.*) Never mind about that. What is all this leading up to?

COLIN. Blackmail. I can smell it a mile off.

JACOB. Where is this letter?

SEBASTIEN. In a strong box in the Royal Bank of Canada. But I have a copy of it.

JACOB. (*Authoritatively.*) Let me see it, please.

SEBASTIEN. No, monsieur. That would be a betrayal of confidence. Also it is very long and contains many irrelevancies of a personal nature. I am, however, perfectly prepared to read you any extracts that are pertinent to the present circumstances.

JACOB. What is the meaning of all this? What are you up to?

SEBASTIEN. I am not up to anything. I am merely embarrassed, for reasons that will be only too apparent later on.

JACOB. Come to the point, please. Read the letter.

SEBASTIEN. (*Looking at* ISOBEL.) Have I madame's permission?

ISOBEL. (*Agitated.*) I suppose so—Jacob—what am I to say?

JACOB. (*To* SEBASTIEN.) You have madame's permission to proceed.

COLIN. There's something shady about this.

JANE. Shut up, Colin.

JACOB. (*Impatiently.*) Go on.

SEBASTIEN. (*With a slight shrug.*) Very well. Actually I would have preferred to read it to you or to your lawyer in private, Monsieur Friedland. However, if you insist, I have no choice. Just a moment. (*In tense silence he produces a wad of papers from his left coat pocket, glances through them, scrutinizing the names or addresses on each of them, doesn't find what he is looking for, and puts them back—takes another wad from his right pocket, goes through them, discovers post card of a nude* woman, slyly shows it to COLIN—and audience—then puts wad back in his pocket, going finally to another wad of papers in his inner pocket, glances through them, extracts a typewritten letter and places the rest carefully back in his pocket. He clears his throat and looks at everyone with a slight smile.*) Ready?

COLIN. For God's sake get on with it.

SEBASTIEN. (*Reading.*) "My dear Sébastien. In case the validity of this personal letter to you should ever be questioned, I will begin it by stating that I am sane and healthy and in full possession of my faculties—" (*He looks up.*) Actually he had a slight head cold at the time, but I gave him two tablets of Benedril, a nice hot toddy, tucked him up in bed—with a friend of his—and piff paff—

JACOB. Never mind about that—go on.

JANE. The news in your letter must be very bad, Sébastien, you are so obviously enjoying yourself.

SEBASTIEN. Not exactly bad, Miss Jane. Shall we say—startling!

JACOB. (*Almost shouting.*) Read it!

SEBASTIEN. (*Continuing to read.*) "In the event of my demise, I have decided to leave no will and testament, for the simple reason that always having spent any money I earned the moment I received it and frequently before I received it, I have nothing to leave to anyone beyond a few personal effects. In recognition of your loyal service to me since July 13th, 1946, I should have liked to have bequeathed you a handsome emolument, or at least to have repaid the two hundred and seventy thousand francs I owe you. However, you will doubtless be able to recover this paltry sum from that stingy old bastard, Jacob Friedland." (*He looks up and smiles deprecatingly.*)

JACOB. (*Grimly.*) Continue.

SEBASTIEN. "The whole of my estate will inevitably revert to my loving wife as a just and fitting recompense for the monumental lack of understanding she has lavished on me since we first met on Armistice night

1918 when, owing to an excess of patriotism and inferior Sauterne, she consented to join her life to mine."

COLIN. (*Protectively*.) Mother, I really think—

ISOBEL. Hush, Colin. I would like to hear the rest of the letter.

JACOB. Perhaps it would be advisable, Isobel, for you to return to the hotel with Pamela and Jane. I can deal with this.

ISOBEL. No, Jacob. My husband's insults, even from beyond the grave, are powerless to hurt me.

COLIN. Good for you, mother.

JACOB. Whatever you wish, my dear. (*To* SEBASTIEN.) Go on.

SEBASTIEN. (*Reading*.) "I am well aware that thanks to Mr. Friedland's unscrupulous business acumen, my canvases have achieved a commercial value grossly out of proportion to their merits. In fairness to him, however, I must state that I have reaped considerable financial benefit from his quite remarkable capacity for deceiving the public. My wife and family, also thanks to him, have received over the years a fair percentage of the profits, although I consider this sop to the laws of matrimony unnecessary as my wife has always enjoyed a more than adequate income of her own"—(*looks up*)—there now comes a rather long dissertation on the iniquities of the marriage and divorce laws. It is quite amusing in a bawdy way. Mr. Sorodin had a rich and varied vocabulary as you may remember. Would you like me to read it or skip to the more important part of the letter, the "clou" as we say in France?

JACOB. (*Tersely*.) Skip it and go on.

SEBASTIEN. Very well. (*He reads in a barely distinguishable undertone*.) "—bla bla bla—Canon Law—bla bla bla—self-centred, sanctimonious hypocrites—bla bla bla—bloody impertinence—bla bla bla—bla bla bla—a bunch of predatory fo—bla bla bla—" Ah here we are. "In consideration of the fact that when this letter is ultimately made public I shall be in my grave, I feel it to be only fair that the world of Art, to which I owe so much, should receive from me one final and unequivocal statement which is, that with the exception of a water colour of an old sheep dog executed at Edinburgh when I was eleven years old, I have never painted a picture of any sort or kind in the whole course of my life."

(ISOBEL *gives a slight cry, puts her hand to her throat and chokes.*)

CURTAIN

ACT TWO

SCENE 1

A few hours have elapsed since Act One.

The CURTAIN rises on a scene of general dejection. ISOBEL *is lying on the sofa with her eyes closed.* COLIN *is sitting with a plate of food.* PAMELA *is sitting gloomily also with a plate of food.* JANE *too is eating.* JACOB *is sitting Down Right.*

JANE. Won't you have some of this pâté, Jacob? It's awfully good.

JACOB. It would choke me.

JANE. You really should try to eat something. Shall I go into the kitchen and ask what's-her-name to scramble some eggs?

COLIN. If the man doesn't want to eat, why badger him?

JANE. He must keep up his strength. Violent shocks to the nervous system are terribly devitalising, besides which he has talked himself into a state of exhaustion.

PAMELA. And a fat lot of good it has done. It would have been much better if we had all gone home hours ago when I suggested it. We shall feel much more able to cope with everything after a good sleep.

JACOB. (*Raising his head.*) A good sleep! Are you mad?

PAMELA. Certainly not. I'm beginning to think that Colin and I are the only sane ones among the lot of you. We always thought Sorodin's pictures were fakes anyway, and said so. Didn't we, Colin?

COLIN. (*With his mouth full.*) Yes, we did.

JACOB. (*With controlled fury.*) Without wishing to be rude, Colin, I must frankly say that, where works of art are concerned, I could never consider you or your wife's opinion to be in the least valid, or even interesting.

COLIN. Here, steady on!

JACOB. Please do not think that this is in any way intended as a reproach. We all aim to be specialists in our own milieu. I have no doubt whatever that you are an expert on military strategy and that your wife is an accomplished horsewoman. I am equally convinced that neither of you could distinguish a Picasso from a hole in the ground.

COLIN. At least we'd know the hole in the ground *was* a hole in the ground. (PAMELA *laughs*.)

JACOB. (*Savagely*.) Well—I wish you'd both find one and fall down it.

COLIN. (*Rising*.) Ha, ha! Bloody funny! (*Returns glass and plate to sofa table*.)

ISOBEL. (*Opening her eyes*.) Colin, you know I don't like you to use that word.

JANE. Do stop baiting Jacob. He's very upset.

PAMELA. I don't see why he should insult Colin and me, however upset he is.

ISOBEL. I wish you'd all stop bickering. My head's splitting.

JACOB. It can't be true. It must be a trick, some low, blackmailing trick. I refuse to believe that it is true.

JANE. Nothing can be proved until you actually see the letter and you can't possibly do that until tomorrow morning because the bank's shut.

JACOB. Do *you* believe it?

JANE. Yes. I'm afraid I do.

JACOB. (*Rising*.) Do you realise what it would mean if that letter got into the Press? Do you realise the full implication of this ghastly situation?

JANE. The letter might be a forgery. We can't tell until the handwriting is identified.

JACOB. Even if it is a forgery my reputation would be ruined for ever if the papers got hold of it.

JANE. We must see to it that they don't.

JACOB. This is a nightmare.

JANE. If it is true that father didn't paint the pictures

it stands to reason that someone else did. The first thing to do is to find out who.

COLIN. Try ringing up the nearest asylum.

JANE. Do be quiet, Colin.

COLIN. It's a very sensible suggestion. Whoever painted "Portrait of Marjorie" must be as mad as a hatter.

PAMELA. (*Giggling.*) Oh, Colin, you do make me laugh sometimes, really you do!

JACOB. I think it would be more helpful if you continued to amuse your wife in the library.

COLIN. We're quite comfortable here, thanks.

JANE. Do you think Sébastien knows who painted them? I know he swore he didn't, but he might have been lying.

COLIN. (*Laughing.*) Perhaps he did them himself.

JACOB. Whoever painted those pictures was a genius. That is my considered opinion. Not only is it my opinion, it is the verdict of all the finest art critics in the civilised world.

JANE. Do art critics really know?

JACOB. Of course they do. They are most of them men of the highest integrity.

ISOBEL. I have often heard you refer to them as sycophantic sheep.

JACOB. Only on the rare occasions when their opinions have run contrary to my own. (*The TELEPHONE rings.*)

ISOBEL. Oh dear! I wonder who that can be.

PAMELA. Probably the Press. (*The TELEPHONE continues to ring. They* ALL *look at it anxiously.*)

ISOBEL. Do you suppose we'd better answer it?

JANE. Ring for Sébastien.

COLIN. I'm surprised he isn't here by now. He generally has his ear clamped to the keyhole. (*The TELEPHONE continues to ring.*) I'll deal with it. (*He goes to the telephone and lifts up the receiver.*) Hallo—hallo.—This is Mr. Sorodin's studio.—What? I beg your pardon.—Parlez-vous Français?—I'm afraid I don't quite understand—WHAT?

SEBASTIEN. (*Comes in from the terrace.*) Excuse me, sir. (*He takes the telephone from* COLIN.) Allô—ici Invalides 2645.—Ah! (*He smiles.*) Aoun choong—nee nee bovoo tchailung—ienfo laou woon tragedy peenoo tialan wang aoueen catastrophe—nee boula maniyar kong gai fanyialouning— Gonk—gonk. (*He hangs up.*)

COLIN. Who the devil was that?

SEBASTIEN. The physical training instructor from the Shanghai branch of the Y.M.C.A. (*He goes out.*)

JANE. You are quite convinced, Jacob, that all father's pictures were painted by one person?

COLIN. Or a chimpanzee with a brush in its mouth.

PAMELA. (*Going into gales of laughter.*) Oh, Colin!

ISOBEL. (*Gently.*) I think, dear, that considering we only laid your father to rest this afternoon, it is not in very good taste to call him a chimpanzee.

COLIN. I didn't. He didn't paint the pictures, anyhow.

JACOB. That has yet to be proved.

JANE. Assuming the worst, that father's letter was true, so far nobody outside this room knows it.

COLIN. Except Sébastien.

JANE. Sébastien can be dealt with.

JACOB. He can sell it to the highest bidder.

JANE. Exactly. We must bid higher.

COLIN. We'll be laying ourselves open to a charge of defrauding the public.

JANE. That can't be helped. The public has been defrauded for years and it might just as well go on being for a little longer.

ISOBEL. I cannot agree to that, Jane. I am sorry, but it is against all my principles.

JANE. Oh, mother, really . . .

JACOB. (*Rising.*) Is it in accordance with your principles to bring ruin and disgrace on a man who has always tried to be your friend?

ISOBEL. What nonsense, Jacob dear. We all know it isn't your fault.

JACOB. It doesn't matter whose fault it is. My whole reputation is in jeopardy!

ISOBEL. Well, you must admit that it was a little silly of you to let Paul pull the wool over your eyes in the first place, wasn't it? I know we're all liable to make mistakes sometimes but surely it's better, once we know we've been wrong, to come bravely out into the open and say so, don't you think?

JACOB. (*With restraint.*) No, Isobel, I do not. Nor have I any intention of coming bravely out into the open and saying that I was wrong when I know with every fibre of my being that I was right. I still maintain that whoever painted those pictures had genius.

ISOBEL. Well, I am afraid that I can't agree with you. When you showed me that first picture of Paul's years ago, it was as much as I could do not to laugh outright, really it was. That awful looking woman with a pot on her head!

JACOB. (*Patiently.*) "Market Woman in Algiers" has been acknowledged to be a masterpiece.

ISOBEL. You still can't convince me that women go to market stark naked, even in Algiers. (COLIN *and* PAMELA *laugh.*)

JANE. This is all rather beside the point, mother. Don't you see that we must stand by Jacob?

ISOBEL. I am very sorry, but my conscience would not permit me to uphold, even for a brief period, what I know to be a lie.

PAMELA. I agree with mother. Let's be honest and above board. It pays in the long run.

JANE. That is exactly what it won't do. If this becomes public, not only will poor Jacob be done for but the whole of father's estate will amount to nothing. We must be practical. What possible good could be achieved by bursting this scandal wide open? Surely it is our first duty to find whoever it was father bribed to ghost-paint for him and then it will be up to Jacob to see that justice is done.

ISOBEL. Justice?

JANE. Of course. Jacob must guarantee that whoever painted the pictures will ultimately get the recognition he deserves. I am right—aren't I, Jacob?

JACOB. Yes, my dear.

ISOBEL. I wish Father Flanagan were here.

JANE. I don't see what he could do if he were.

ISOBEL. I know that you don't like Father Flanagan, Jane, but you can take my word for it, he is a very wonderful man; almost a mystic.

JANE. What we need at the moment is a clairvoyant.

COLIN. For once I agree with Jane.

ISOBEL. (*Reproachfully.*) Oh, Colin!

COLIN. Even dear old Mr. Flint would be a damned sight more useful than Father Flanagan. He may not be a clairvoyant but he is a trained lawyer.

ISOBEL. Dear old Mr. Flint wanted to come with us but he couldn't leave his wife.

JANE. Unlike father.

ISOBEL. For shame, Jane.

PAMELA. Why don't we telephone to dear old Mr. Flint and put all our cards on the table?

JACOB. (*With dreadful calm.*) I can explain to you why we cannot telephone to dear old Mr. Flint, or to Father Flanagan, or to the Pope. It is because we have all agreed not to divulge what has happened to a living soul.

COLIN. Mother hasn't.

JACOB. You must agree, Isobel. I implore you to agree. If Mr. Flint knew, his partners would know, and if his partners knew, his partners' wives would know, and before we knew where we were, the secret would be out and in the papers.

ISOBEL. You have a curious idea of the probity of English lawyers.

JACOB. I have a very definite idea of the incapacity of the human race to keep its mouth shut.

COLIN. This isn't getting us anywhere. Why don't we all go back to the hotel?

ACT II NUDE WITH VIOLIN 37

(SEBASTIEN *enters by service door.*)

SEBASTIEN. (*To* JACOB.) Did you ring, sir?
JACOB. No, I did not.
SEBASTIEN. How strange. I could have sworn I heard a bell. Perhaps it was Notre Dame. Is there anything I can do for you?
JANE. Yes, Sébastian, a great deal.
SEBASTIEN. At your service always, miss.
COLIN. Oh Lord! We're off again!
JANE. You said some while ago that father's letter was witnessed by Marie-Céleste and a head waiter.
SEBASTIEN. Jules Messonier, 80 bis rue de Perpignan.
JANE. Can he speak English?
SEBASTIEN. Oh, no. I believe he picked up a little American during the liberation, but only a few idiomatic words such as okay and demi-tasse.
JANE. He didn't read the letter? They neither of them read it?
SEBASTIEN. No, they only signed it as witnesses.
JANE. Good. To your certain knowledge no one outside this room knows its contents.
SEBASTIEN. To my certain knowledge. I deposited it in the bank myself in a sealed package.
JANE. Had you any suspicion, when you first entered my father's employ, that he wasn't a painter at all?
SEBASTIEN. None, Miss Jane. He explained to me that complete solitude was essential to him when he was working. That was the reason he gave for never painting in this studio. He said it was merely a façade to impress the dealers. Later, of course, when he knew me better, he took me into his confidence.
JANE. Where did he work, then, or pretend to work?
SEBASTIEN. St. Cloud. He rented a studio there under a false name. He used to leave here in the morning gay as a lark and return in the evening exhausted.
JANE. Every morning?
SEBASTIEN. Oh, no! Only when, as he said, he felt the urge.

JACOB. St. Cloud? Where in St. Cloud?
SEBASTIEN. 16 Impasse de Louis Philippe.
JACOB. Why didn't you tell us this before?
SEBASTIEN. You never asked me.
JACOB. Have you the keys?
SEBASTIEN. Yes, monsieur.
JACOB. Where are they?
SEBASTIEN. With the letter in the Royal Bank of Canada.
JACOB. Is the studio empty? Is there anything in it?
SEBASTIEN. Only Sorodin's remaining canvas.
JACOB. (*Almost screaming.*) What!!!
SEBASTIEN. His last great masterpiece, "Nude With Violin." (*The FRONT DOOR BELL rings.*) Excuse me. (*He bows and goes out.*)
JACOB. (*Wildly and rising.*) Remaining canvas! "Nude With Violin"!
JANE. Keep calm, Jacob, for heaven's sake, keep calm.
JACOB. The cunning blackmailing scoundrel! I'll have him arrested, I'll have him flung into gaol!

(*There is the SOUND of RAISED VOICES outside.*)

JANE. Jacob! Pull yourself together. You *must* pull yourself together.
CLINTON. (*Bursts into the room. He is followed by SEBASTIEN.*) Forgive me for intruding, but I've just had a cable from my editor.
JACOB. I don't care if you've had a cable from John Foster Dulles. Please go away.
CLINTON. It's urgent. It's about Sorodin. Where is it?
JANE. Where is what?
CLINTON. Sorodin's posthumous masterpiece, the greatest picture he ever painted. (*He produces a cable from his pocket.*) The cable says it's called "Rude With Violin."
SEBASTIEN. The intuition of the Western Union is almost uncanny.
CLINTON. The news broke in New York yesterday. All

the dealers are crazy with excitement. Elmore P. Riskin, the director of the Manhattan Museum of Modern Art, has hopped a plane and is arriving tomorrow. You must let me see it, Mr. Friedland. *Life* Magazine is prepared to carry it on the cover page in colour.

JACOB. (*Brokenly.*) Go away, Mr. Clinton Preminger, junior, just go away.

CLINTON. Oh, please—please—I implore you to let me see it! It may make the whole difference to my approach.

COLIN. Approach to what?

CLINTON. Everything!

JANE. Mr. Friedland is very upset, Mr. Preminger. Please do as he asks and go away. It is quite out of the question for you to see the picture.

CLINTON. But why—why?

SEBASTIEN. It's being varnished.

JANE. Thank you, Sébastien.

CLINTON. This is terribly important to me.

SEBASTIEN. It is terribly important to all of us, monsieur. (*The FRONT DOOR BELL rings.*) Excuse me. (*He goes out.*)

CLINTON. (*To* ISOBEL.) Mrs. Sorodin, I appeal to you—

JANE. Mr. Preminger—you really must stop appealing to my mother, it flusters her.

COLIN. Now see here, Preminger—

JANE. Just a moment, Colin. I will try to arrange for you to see the picture in the morning.

CLINTON. Do you think it will be dry?

JANE. I can't promise anything but if you will go away quietly now I assure you that I will do all I can.

CLINTON. Okay. I'm sorry—I'll go. Good-bye. (*He goes out quickly.*)

ISOBEL. Americans are curious, aren't they? So abrupt!

JACOB. What are we to do now? If New York had the news yesterday, London will have had it today. I shall have all the English dealers pestering the life out of me— Alaric Craigie, Beddington, probably the Tooths.

ISOBEL. What on earth have teeth got to do with it?

SEBASTIEN. (*Re-enters.*) A Princess Pavlikov has called, Mr. Friedland. She seems agitated.

JACOB. A Princess who?

SEBASTIEN. Pavlikov. As the name implies, she is a Russian.

JACOB. Send her away. I can't possibly see anyone now.

SEBASTIEN. (*Meaningly.*) I think, in the circumstances, that it would be wise to grant her a brief interview.

JACOB. What do you mean?

SEBASTIEN. She says she is a very old friend of Mr. Sorodin's. She apparently knew him many many years ago, during his Farouche period.

ISOBEL. (*Rising.*) I really don't feel up to meeting any more strangers at the moment—Colin—Pamela— (PAMELA *rises.*)

JANE. (*Firmly.*) Show her in, Sébastien.

SEBASTIEN. Volontiers, mademoiselle. (*He goes out.*)

ISOBEL. Really, Jane, you are being very highhanded. I don't know what has come over you. You've been ordering us about and shouting at us all day long like—like a sergeant-major.

JANE. Please sit down again, darling. This woman may be able to help us—don't you see?

SEBASTIEN. (*Re-enters, announcing.*) Princess Pavlikov. (*He stands aside and* ANYA PAVLIKOV *comes in. She is a woman of about fifty. Her face is a trifle ravaged but her make-up is excellent. She is discreetly dressed but her jewellery, if it were real, would be worth a fortune.*)

ANYA. (*To* JACOB.) Mr. Friedland?

JACOB. I am Jacob Friedland.

ANYA. Ah, yes. I see now that you could not be anyone else.

JACOB. (*Stiffly.*) I fear I don't understand.

ANYA. (*With a charming smile.*) It is no matter. (*She looks at* ISOBEL.) This lady—you will please make presentation?

JACOB. Mrs. Paul Sorodin.

ISOBEL. (*Nodding.*) How do you do.

ANYA. Of course, I see also that you could not be anyone else. (*She sees* COLIN.) My God!
COLIN. I beg your pardon?
ANYA. (*To* COLIN.) Eyes! Not mouth. Mouth is different, but eyes!
JANE. I am Jane Sorodin. This is my brother Colin, and this is his wife.
ANYA. (*Looking raptly at* PAMELA.) Beautiful! Quite, quite beautiful! The true English mould. Magnificent!
PAMELA. (*Embarrassed.*) Thank you.
ANYA. (*Dreamily.*) Florence Nightingale, Gainsborough. Clive of India, what a country! I really must sit down. (*Sits.*)
JANE. Please do.
ANYA. Is there brandy in house?
SEBASTIEN. Perhaps Madame la Princesse would prefer vodka?
ANYA. (*Violently.*) No, no, no! I cannot bear vodka. It makes me gay and noisy for a small while then suddenly tears come and regret and despair fill heart. It is most beastly. Brandy is better, especially after journey.
SEBASTIEN. Very good, madame. (*He goes out by service door, staring at* ANYA *as he goes.*)
ANYA. That man has coloured blood. You can tell by his cheek-bones. (*Looking at* ISOBEL.) You are devoted to him?
JANE. We hardly know him. He was my father's servant.
ANYA. Ah. Do not trust him.
COLIN. Thanks. We don't.
JACOB. I understand that you wished to see me urgently.
ANYA. I do. Most urgently. But it is delicate matter, perhaps there is tiny bathroom where we talk privately?
JACOB. Does it concern the late Paul Sorodin?
ANYA. Oh, yes.
JACOB. In that case it also concerns everyone in this room. You may speak freely.

ANYA. Ah! You wish me to say what I say before witnesses. Is idea that?

JANE. (*Tactfully.*) Not exactly. (ANYA *lights a cigarette and throws match over her shoulder.*) You see, we are all most anxious to discover as much as possible about my father's earlier years. As you may know he left my mother in 1925 and we have had no actual contact with him since.

ISOBEL. I cannot feel, Jane, that our private family affairs can be of any interest to Princess Pav—Pav—

ANYA. (*Laughing gayly.*) No Pav-Pav. Pavlikov. It is what you call maiden name. I took it back when my husband showed true colours and went to Düsseldorf with my cousin Masha. He was heartless pig called Flanagan.

JANE. Oh dear!

ANYA. Irish.

PAMELA. (*Helpfully.*) In Ireland Flanagan is a very common name.

ANYA. He was very common man.

SEBASTIEN. (*Re-enters with a balloon glass of brandy on a salver.*) Kniagynia, vashe cognac. (Your brandy, Madame la Princesse.)

ANYA. (*Taking it.*) Spasibo. Pochemou vi ne skazali chto vsia cemia zdez? (*Soft* C.) (Thank you. Why didn't you say the whole family was here?)

SEBASTIEN. Ia doumal chto loutshe vam samoy oubeditsia. (I thought you'd better see for yourself.)

ANYA. Vi mugli predoupredit (*soft*) menia. (You could have warned me.)

SEBASTIEN. Mne kazaloc chto eto ne mayo delo. (I did not consider it any of my business.)

JACOB. That will be all, Sébastien.

SEBASTIEN. (*Crossing to service door.*) Very good, monsieur. (*With meaning.*) I shall be just outside the door as usual if you should need me. (*He bows and goes out.*)

ANYA. He speaks good Russian but bad accent. Ukraine—harsh on ear. Has he ever been in prison?

COLIN. Frequently, I should think.

ANYA. It always gives people a certain "air." Of course many of my family were in prison from time to time but only for political reason. My uncle Sergei used to tell us wonderful prison tales when we were children in Pinsk. He once trained mouse to do little dance. La la la—so, he would say—La la la—so! and it would get up on tiny legs and go round and round—how we laughed!

JACOB. Yes! I am sure it must have been most entertaining, Princess Pavlikov, but we are very eager to hear whatever you have to tell us about Paul Sorodin. It is getting late, and we are all rather tired.

ANYA. (*Putting her cigarette out.*) Very well! Business. (*She looks at* ISOBEL.) You will not mind if I speak truth, Mrs. Sorodin? It is all long ago but I would not wish to wound your heart.

ISOBEL. Please go on. I am fully prepared for whatever revelations you care to make.

ANYA. (*Enthusiastically.*) Fabulous! Wonderful! What a country! What a race! Sir Walter Raleigh, William Pitt, Christina Rossetti—

JACOB. (*Irritably.*) Please say what you have to say, Princess. You knew Sorodin?

ANYA. Yes. (*She sighs wistfully.*) Oh yes, I knew him.

JACOB. Well?

ANYA. How well can one really know anyone? We are all strangers really, lonely strangers groping about in dark. We know face, we know body, we know hands, but soul! That is a thing most different, no?

JACOB. Yes, most different. Therefore we needn't discuss it at the moment, need we? When did you know him?

ANYA. He was my lover from 1925 until 1929.

JACOB. Where did you first meet?

ANYA. Here, in Paris. I was a student at École des Beaux Arts, he trod on my foot in Métro and I bit him.

PAMELA. Bit him?

ANYA. Oh yes! I always bite people when I am suddenly astonished.

JACOB. What were you studying at the Beaux Arts?

ANYA. Sculpture. Feeling of clay intoxicates me. I go quite mad sometimes and dance and shout very loud. (*Laughs.*)

JACOB. When did you start painting?

ANYA. (*Startled.*) Painting! So you know? You have known all the time. You have been most slyboots.

JACOB. I don't *know* anything, but I want to. I want to know all that you can tell me. It may be of vital importance.

ANYA. It was Sorodin who made me give up the sculpting. Clay drove him crazy, all over house nothing but clay. Then one day we have great great drama and he throw it all in sea, so I leave him in Algiers and go over mountains to Bou-Sada in desert.

JANE. Algiers!

ANYA. (*To* JACOB.) Have you ever been Bou-Sada?

JACOB. No, I have not.

ANYA. Well, don't go. It's ruined now.

JACOB. (*Persevering.*) When did you start painting?

ANYA. When Sorodin came to find me and we were lovers again and live in house in La Napoule.

JACOB. (*Striking his forehead.*) La Napoule!

ANYA. You remember now?

JANE. (*Eagerly.*) Remember what?

ANYA. Mr. Friedland first meet Sorodin in La Napoule. I had gone market one day, and when I come back in evening all those silly, silly paintings Sorodin make me do are no more there.

JACOB. Oh, my God!

ANYA. Mr. Friedland buy all paintings except two, one of lemons hanging from chandelier, and other triangular fish head on cushion. I did fish painting with nail scissors because I had broken brush.

JACOB. (*Sepulchrally.*) It is now in the Chicago Museum of Modern Art.

ANYA. What happened to stupid old lemons?

JACOB. It is the treasured possession of one of the greatest connoisseurs in Buenos Aires.

ANYA. (*Laughing.*) It is great joke, no?

JACOB. No.
ANYA. Sorodin would laugh if he alive now.
COLIN. I'll bet he would!
JANE. How many paintings did you do for my father altogether?
ANYA. I cannot remember, darling, but many—great, great many. He made me go on and on and on. That was why I leave him really. He thought it was because I love darling Egmont, but really it was smell of turpentine. (*To* ISOBEL.) You like turpentine smell?
ISOBEL. (*Flurried.*) Well—no—I suppose I don't actually. I mean—I don't really know.
ANYA. After long while painting believe me it make feel terrible.
JACOB. You left Sorodin and went away with this—this Egmont?
ANYA. That is truth.
JACOB. And you never painted again?
ANYA. (*Gaily.*) Oh, my God, no! Egmont hate painting. Egmont mechanic.
COLIN. Good for Egmont.
ANYA. We start garage near Grenoble, fine business, many tourists, Route Napoléon.
JACOB. Did Sorodin try to prevent you leaving him?
ANYA. Oh yes. For three weeks we have the scenes. Sorodin wish kill Egmont, Egmont wish kill Sorodin. I cry, everyone cry, then Sorodin give in and make me sign letter.
JACOB. Letter?
ANYA. Yes. I have copy here in bag. True letter in Swiss Bank Brussels. Egmont witness letter. Then everyone shake hands, drink cognac, and we go.
JACOB. Is Egmont alive?
ANYA. I think no. He went Belgian Congo 1934 to have better garage, but Belgian Congo bad business for garage. Mosquitoes, Tsee Tsee flies, Albert Schweitzer—what a country!
JACOB. Was the letter a form of contract? Did Sorodin pay you money?

ANYA. Oh yes. Every year until war. Then no more.

JACOB. Please show me the letter.

ANYA. Certainly. (*Hands it to him.*) True letter in Sorodin's handwriting. Typed copy more easy to understand.

JACOB. (*Reading it.*) This is appalling!

COLIN. What's in the letter? Is it in English?

JACOB. (*Still reading it.*) Yes—yes, it's in English.

JANE. Tell us the worst, Jacob.

JACOB. The gist of it is that Madame Pavlikov agrees to renounce all claims on her paintings. She also swears solemnly in the presence of witnesses never to speak or write of the transaction to a living person. In return for this Sorodin guarantees to pay her an annuity of three hundred thousand francs, to be paid into her account in the National Bank of Switzerland in Brussels.

COLIN. Why Brussels?

ANYA. My stepmother had little business there.

JANE. What sort of business?

ANYA. It is difficult to explain, but it was good until war, then *pouf!* everything break in small pieces—my stepmother die—girls all run away.

COLIN. (*To* ANYA.) Girls?

ANYA. My step-sisters.

JANE. And you, where did you go?

ANYA. Dublin. Ireland neutral country. That's where I meet Flanagan. But I come back after war to Brussels—then Flanagan leave me. I try to find Sorodin, no Sorodin. Then at last I come here again and find Sorodin.

JACOB. When?

ANYA. Five years ago. He shout at me. I bite him. He give me million francs. I take, and now he dies.

COLIN. A million francs! That's a thousand pounds, isn't it?

ANYA. Exchange most lousy.

JACOB. How much do you want, Madame Pavlikov?

ANYA. Money vulgar. I prefer not discuss.

JACOB. You realise of course that this letter is not in any way legal?

ANYA. Not legal maybe but most fine joke for Press.
JACOB. How much do you want?
ANYA. I will ask lawyer.
JACOB. (*Angrily.*) You will do no such thing!
JANE. Hush, Jacob, I am sure we will be able to come to some reasonable arrangement with Princess Pavlikov.
JACOB. This is sheer blackmail!
ANYA. (*To* JACOB.) It is business, Mr. Friedland.
JACOB. If you will deliver the original of this letter to me at my office, number 506 Boulevard Haussmann within three days, I will draw up a contract guaranteeing you five hundred thousand francs a year for the rest of your life.
ISOBEL. Jacob!
COLIN. (*Horrified.*) The man's barmy!
JACOB. Be quiet and leave this to me. (*To* ANYA.) Well?
ANYA. Belgian francs?
JACOB. Certainly not, French francs.
ANYA. Then no agree. French francs most shifty. Up one day, down next, Government change—wallop!
SEBASTIEN. (*Enters from service door.*) You rang, monsieur?
JACOB. No, I did not.
SEBASTIEN. How extraordinary! I made sure I heard a bell. It must have been a tinkling piano in the next apartment. (*To* ANYA.) Madame would like me to escort her to her car?
COLIN. Car?
SEBASTIEN. Yes, monsieur. I have been having a little chat with madame's chauffeur. A most interesting man.
ANYA. (*Sharply.*) What have you said—you and chauffeur?
SEBASTIEN. We found we had a great deal in common.
ANYA. (*To* JACOB.) The offer you make just now. It is definite?
JACOB. Yes.
ANYA. Then I accept.
SEBASTIEN. Excuse me, Mr. Friedland, Madame Soro-

din, but I venture to suggest that it is a little late in the evening to make final decisions. In the morning when the brain is clearer and the sun is shining, matters, even business matters, assume quite a different aspect.

ANYA. He make offer before witnesses. I accept before witnesses. No more fiddle-faddle—it is settled!

SEBASTIEN. It is not settled!

ANYA. (*Visibly agitated, rising.*) You and chauffeur—what was said between you?

SEBASTIEN. Ia vass predoupredill ne otkrivat (*soft* t) rta. (I warned you not to open your mouth too wide.)

ANYA. Chto vi skazali? (What have you said?)

SEBASTIEN. Eto mayo delo. (That's my business.)

ANYA. Vi ljiote, e vi niskaia svinia! (You are low, lying pig!)

SEBASTIEN. Molchat (*soft* t) ouhodite. Esli vi oumeite sebia derjat (*soft* t) dlia vas eto boudette gorazdo polesnie. (Shut up and get out. You'll be fairly treated if you behave yourself.)

COLIN. What the hell's going on?

JACOB. What is all this, Sébastien? Kindly explain—in English.

ANYA. You not listen! He stinking half-breed liar!

ISOBEL. Oh dear, I do hope there isn't going to be any unpleasantness!

ANYA. I told you not trust him. Look cheek-bones!

JACOB. What were you saying just now? Tell me the truth, please.

SEBASTIEN. Willingly, monsieur. I was merely explaining to Madame la Princesse that it was foolish to open her mouth too wide and that she would be fairly treated if she behaved herself and got the hell out of here.

JACOB. Have you ever met her before?

SEBASTIEN. No, monsieur.

JANE. You weren't here when she called on my father some years back?

SEBASTIEN. Alas no, miss. I happened to be staying with friends in Barbizon for the week-end. On my return, however, I gathered that a fairly stormy interview had taken place.

JACOB. How did you gather that?

SEBASTIEN. Marie-Céleste was hysterical, Mr. Sorodin's left arm was severely lacerated, and the sofa had been sent away to be re-covered.

ANYA. (*Almost frantic.*) You and chauffeur—what you talk about? Tell me swiftly.

SEBASTIEN. The past.

JACOB. The past—what do you mean?

SEBASTIEN. I have a bottle of Armagnac in my room—it was a birthday present from Mr. Sorodin. I cannot bear to drink alone, and Marie-Céleste has gone to bed, so I invited madame's chauffeur to share it with me.

JACOB. Come to the point, please. You knew this man before?

SEBASTIEN. Oh yes. Egmont and I are old friends.

JANE. Egmont?

SEBASTIEN. Yes, Egmont Vasquier. He was a garage mechanic, a bluff, cheerful fellow but inclined to become violent when crossed in any way. He was also a trifle unscrupulous in regard to money. That's really what they jugged him for.

COLIN. Jugged him?

SEBASTIEN. Oh yes. That is how we first met, in the late thirties. By the strangest coincidence we happened to occupy the same prison cell—in the Belgian Congo.

ANYA. You are a dirty filthy blackguardly peasant. Your accent stinks like the fish market in Odessa, and if my great Uncle Vladimir Pavlickovitch were here he would send you bouncing, bouncing in a mule cart to the salt mines of Siberia. Pig, pig, pig.

(SEBASTIEN *and* ANYA *scream at each other in Russian.* ANYA *bites* SEBASTIEN *as he pushes her off stage.* ANYA *screams,* SEBASTIEN, *with great aplomb, turns back into the room as*)

THE CURTAIN FALLS

ACT TWO

Scene 2

The time is about five o'clock on the following afternoon.

When the CURTAIN rises, SEBASTIEN is on stage. MARIE-CELESTE enters.

MARIE-CELESTE. Il y a cet Américain à la porte encore.
SEBASTIEN. Qu'est-ce qu'il demande?
MARIE-CELESTE. Vous. Il est agité.
SEBASTIEN. Il est toujours agité. Dis que je suis sorti.
CLINTON. (*Enters abruptly.*) Forgive me for busting in like this, but I'm in trouble.
SEBASTIEN. What sort of trouble?
CLINTON. Bad trouble. Buddy Carmichael's in town.
SEBASTIEN. Who the hell is Buddy Carmichael?
CLINTON. He's covering the Sorodin story for *Look*. If he gets his piece in before mine I'm sunk.
MARIE-CELESTE. Qu'est-ce qu'il dit, le pauvre?
SEBASTIEN. Rien d'importance. Sauve toi.
MARIE-CELESTE. Il est un brave type, sois gentil avec lui. Il est tellement nerveux.
SEBASTIEN. (*Firmly.*) Va t'en.
MARIE-CELESTE. Ah! Bien! Ce n'est pas juste! Maintenant, que ça devient interessant, on me renvoie. Va-t-en! Va-t-en! Qu'on me dit. Je proteste. (*Etc. Goes out angrily.*)
CLINTON. Is it dry yet?
SEBASTIEN. What on earth are you talking about?
CLINTON. Sorodin's last picture, of course. You said it was being varnished. Is it dry yet?
SEBASTIEN. It's tacky.
CLINTON. I've had another cable from my editor. I've got to write a description of it.
SEBASTIEN. You'll have to wait. In any case it is virtually indescribable. Like all masterpieces. How can mere

words possibly convey the inherent quality, the intrinsic significance of a great painting? Would you, for instance, have the temerity to send your editor a telegraphic analysis of the Mona Lisa?

CLINTON. Of course I wouldn't. Anyway, as far as *Life* Magazine is concerned, the Mona Lisa is Old Hat.

SEBASTIEN. Old Hat! May God forgive you!

CLINTON. Well, you know what I mean.

SEBASTIEN. How could you with—if I may say so— your fairly limited vocabulary—find words to express the eternal mystery of that smile? That secret smile that has brooded slyly over so many, many turbulent years— so many, many generations of men. How—

CLINTON. (*Slightly rebellious.*) I wouldn't try. I don't care for the Mona Lisa anyway.

SEBASTIEN. Neither do I.

CLINTON. Good for you! What did Sorodin think of the Mona Lisa?

SEBASTIEN. He said she looked as though she had just been sick or was about to be.

CLINTON. (*Enthusiastically.*) Gee that's wonderful! I must write it down. (*He finds a piece of paper in his pocket and scribbles on it.*)

SEBASTIEN. Mr. Sorodin lacked reverence to an alarming degree, and, like so many geniuses, his criticisms were liable to be prejudiced by his own very definite likes and dislikes.

CLINTON. Tell me about his likes and dislikes.

SEBASTIEN. I haven't time at the moment.

CLINTON. What did he think of Picasso?

SEBASTIEN. He tried not to.

CLINTON. Was he musical?

SEBASTIEN. Tone deaf.

CLINTON. No kidding.

SEBASTIEN. He couldn't distinguish between "Begin the Beguine" and "God Save the Queen." He used to make me play them to him over and over again, but it was no good. He invariably rose to his feet for "Begin the Beguine."

CLINTON. Did he ever go to the theatre or the movies?

SEBASTIEN. He only really liked Biblical films. He saw "The Sign of the Cross" seventeen times.

CLINTON. What about ballet?

SEBASTIEN. Dancing in any form nauseated him.

CLINTON. Why?

SEBASTIEN. In the first place he said that watching people turn round and round very fast made him giddy and in the second place he loathed swans.

CLINTON. There are ballets without swans.

SEBASTIEN. Very few.

CLINTON. Tell me more about him, Sébastien—intimate, personal things.

SEBASTIEN. (*Offering* CLINTON *a cigarette.*) Cigarette?

CLINTON. Gee, where did you get that?

SEBASTIEN. Mr. Sorodin gave it to me last Easter in a chocolate egg.

CLINTON. It means so much to me to be able to talk to you, you who were so close to him, who knew his every mood, every facet of his brilliant mind. Tell me about his complexes for instance, his frustrations, his inner compulsions. What was his sex pattern?

SEBASTIEN. Convulsive.

CLINTON. Did he fall in and out of love easily? Was he lonely? Was he melancholic? Was he superstitious?

SEBASTIEN. He never slept thirteen in a bed.

CLINTON. Now you're laughing at me again.

SEBASTIEN. Your very exuberance invites a certain amount of ridicule, Mr. Preminger.

CLINTON. Well, be a pal and lay off it. I'm feeling low.

SEBASTIEN. Cheer up. It's always darkest before dawn.

CLINTON. You've got to let me see that picture, Sébastien, before anyone else does. You've just got to.

SEBASTIEN. Do relax, Mr. Preminger.

CLINTON. Call me Clint. All my pals do.

SEBASTIEN. If only you'll go away I'll call you anything you like—even Clint.

CLINTON. Promise me you won't let anyone see that picture before I do.

SEBASTIEN. I can't promise anything.
CLINTON. (*Seizing him by the arms.*) Please, Sébastien, please—it means everything in the world to me.
SEBASTIEN. (*Struggling slightly to extricate himself.*) Now look here, Mr. Preminger—
CLINTON. Clint.
SEBASTIEN. (*Breaking free.*) All right, if you insist—Clint.
CLINTON. I could use a drink, I'm shot to hell.
SEBASTIEN. Scotch?
CLINTON. Yeah—on the rocks. I didn't sleep a wink last night.
SEBASTIEN. Oh, Clint, I'm surprised at you. What time did you get to bed?
CLINTON. (*Ruefully.*) Five o'clock.
SEBASTIEN. (*Putting ice cubes in a glass.*) What on earth were you doing until five o'clock in the morning?
CLINTON. Oh, you know—the usual thing.
SEBASTIEN. (*Pouring out a generous portion of whisky and bringing it to him.*) I can hazard a guess, but with visiting Americans "the usual thing" is variable.
CLINTON. (*With slight truculence.*) Are visiting Americans so very different from visiting Englishmen and Germans and Italians?
SEBASTIEN. Certainly.
CLINTON. In what way?
SEBASTIEN. They have more money to spend and less knowledge of how to spend it.
CLINTON. I suppose that you, as a European, despise Americans?
SEBASTIEN. Why should you suppose any such thing?
CLINTON. I read a piece in a magazine. It was called—
SEBASTIEN. You mustn't believe everything you read in magazines. In any case I haven't time at the moment to embark on a discussion of international ethics.
CLINTON. Did Sorodin depise Americans?
SEBASTIEN. No, but he definitely despised journalistic generalisations.
CLINTON. You want to know something?

SEBASTIEN. Not particularly.

CLINTON. That clipped British accent of yours slays me.

SEBASTIEN. Does it indeed?

CLINTON. You know I could listen to you talking all day.

SEBASTIEN. Maybe you could, but you're certainly not going to. Finish up your drink now and go away, I have a great deal to do.

CLINTON. Okay. (*He finishes his drink and rises.*) You do like me, don't you?

SEBASTIEN. Absence, Clint, makes the heart grow fonder.

CLINTON. (*Clapping* SEBASTIEN *on the back.*) You're a great guy, Sébastien, and don't forget our dinner date. Boy, I bet you can show me things in Paris that I never even knew existed. So long, Pal. (*Goes out. The TELEPHONE rings.*)

SEBASTIEN. (*At telephone.*) Allô—ici Invalides 2645—Ah, Mr. Friedland—Yes, it is all arranged, the camion will be at St. Cloud the first thing in the morning. I will be there myself to supervise everything and return here in it with the canvas.—Certainly, sir, you may rely on me.—Yes, sir, a short while ago. Mr. Elmore P. Riskin is at the Lancaster and Sir Alaric Craigie at the Crillon, I told them both that you would communicate with them personally. Oh yes, sir, the interview went off most satisfactorily—Madame la Princesse became rather violent at one moment and attempted to bite my thigh, but I—No, sir, my thigh—but Egmont and I managed to calm her down. Egmont is a very sensible man, and is perfectly prepared to settle for French francs, unlike myself who prefers a more stable currency such as dollars. Pray keep calm, Mr. Friedland. Think of your cholesterol. Yes, they both went back to Brussels on the afternoon plane and will return to Paris tomorrow with the document. Yes, sir—not at all, sir— In about half an hour? Very good, sir. (*With a smile he hangs up the receiver. There is a ring at the FRONT DOOR BELL. He rises from the desk, glances round the room to see that everything is in order.* JANE *enters.*)

JANE. Good afternoon, Sébastien.

SEBASTIEN. Good afternoon, Miss Jane.

JANE. I came on before the others because I wanted to have a little talk with you.

SEBASTIEN. I am both flattered and charmed, Miss Jane. Can I offer you any refreshment?

JANE. No, thank you.

SEBASTIEN. A cigarette, perhaps?

JANE. I have my own thank you.

SEBASTIEN. A light at least? (*He lights her cigarette.*)

JANE. Perhaps you would like to sit down?

SEBASTIEN. Mademoiselle is most democratic. But if Marie-Céleste should come in and find me lolling about in the presence of my late employer's daughter, it might undermine her morale.

JANE. I suspect that in this particular establishment Marie-Céleste's morale has survived worse shocks than that.

SEBASTIEN. It's certainly had a few jolts.

JANE. In any case I didn't ask you to loll about, I asked you to sit down.

SEBASTIEN. I am over-ruled. (*He sits.*)

JANE. (*Offering cigarette to* SEBASTIEN, *who takes it.*) Now then—

SEBASTIEN. I am all attention, Miss Jane.

JANE. I don't doubt that for a moment. You strike me as being a very alert character.

SEBASTIEN. Correct.

JANE. Also, a fairly unscrupulous one.

SEBASTIEN. Mademoiselle is too kind.

JANE. Will you answer one question absolutely honestly?

SEBASTIEN. That rather depends what the question is.

JANE. Were you genuinely fond of my father?

SEBASTIEN. (*Quietly, after a slight pause.*) Yes, Miss Jane. I was. You may really believe that.

JANE. (*With a smile.*) Thank you, Sébastien. I do. I

too was fond of him in my own mind although I can barely remember him. My mother accuses me of taking a romantic view of him. Am I wrong?

SEBASTIEN. Of course not. You would have adored him; and if I may say so, I know that he would have adored you. He was a man of remarkable character. Full of charm, vitality and irrepressible humour. Also he was devoted to pleasure, which in Christian communities is always suspect.

JANE. Why did he perpetuate this gigantic hoax?

SEBASTIEN. Because he was the victim of an obsession that tormented him all his life.

JANE. What sort of obsession?

SEBASTIEN. A fanatical, burning hatred of dishonesty.

JANE. You can hardly expect me to believe that when his whole career was founded on a deliberate lie.

SEBASTIEN. Nevertheless, it is true. He loathed cant, jargon, intellectual snobism and the commercialising of creative talent. Successful art-dealers, critics and so-called experts were his *bêtes noires*. His detestation of them was almost pathological.

JANE. But why? Why should he have minded so much?

SEBASTIEN. Creative talent was his god. He worshipped it ardently, passionately, all the more perhaps because he knew he hadn't a vestige of it himself. Far and away above everything else, he loved good painting.

JANE. If he loved good painting so much, how could he possibly have done what he did?

SEBASTIEN. He was a crusader.

JANE. Crusader? Really, Sébastien!

SEBASTIEN. What I am telling you is the truth, Miss Jane.

JANE. It is hard to believe.

SEBASTIEN. Please try. It is most important.

JANE. Why?

SEBASTIEN. Because of all your family you are the only one he would have wanted to share the joke with him.

JANE. How can you possibly know that?

SEBASTIEN. Because I knew him, probably better than

anyone else, and because since yesterday, I have had the privilege of knowing you.
JANE. Thank you, Sébastien.
SEBASTIEN. (*Rising.*) Have I convinced you?
JANE. There is still a great deal that I find difficult to understand. Why, for instance, should he have gone to all the trouble and expense of paying that Russian woman to paint his pictures for him when he could quite easily have done them himself?
SEBASTIEN. If he had painted them himself they would no longer have been fakes.
JANE. How do you mean?
SEBASTIEN. Mr. Friedland and all the nabobs of the art world would have been able to uphold their verdict that he was a genius in spite of any protestations he might make to the contrary. Indeed they would have probably used his protestations to prove their point.
JANE. How could they?
SEBASTIEN. By saying that he was a genius whether he knew it or not and like so many other men of abnormal creative power, unbalanced!
JANE. That letter you read out to us with such unmistakable pleasure. Did you persuade him to write it?
SEBASTIEN. (*Laughing.*) Persuade him? It was the culmination of his life's ambition. It was his final gesture, a last decisive blow aimed at the parasites who, in his opinion, had betrayed the only thing he really respected in human nature, the creative instinct.
JANE. Thank you so much for clarifying the situation for me—at least a little.
SEBASTIEN. You are still not convinced?
JANE. I still believe you know a good deal more than you pretend to know.
SEBASTIEN. How right you are, Miss Jane. But we are friends, aren't we?
JANE. (*Rising and holding out hand with a smile.*) Yes, Sébastien. (*They shake hands.*) We are friends. But there is still one question that is puzzling me.
SEBASTIEN. What is it?

JANE. Princess Pavlikov left my father in 1929. Who painted the rest of his pictures?

SEBASTIEN. In the idiom of our American cousins, Miss Jane—"search me"!

JANE. Oh dear. Poob Jacob. I really am very sorry for him.

SEBASTIEN. (*Smiling.*) Mr. Friedland is certainly in a most unenviable position. We must all do everything we can to help him, mustn't we?

JANE. You don't like Mr. Friedland, do you, Sébastien?

SEBASTIEN. I share your father's opinion of him. He said he was a pompous, plausible, double-crossing old weasel.

JANE. You don't think he knows anything about painting?

SEBASTIEN. I don't think that anyone knows about painting any more. Art, like human nature, has got out of hand. (*There is the SOUND of VOICES in the hall.*)

JANE. Here they are.

SEBASTIEN. I didn't hear the bell.

(CHERRY-MAY WATERTON *enters, followed by* FABRICE. CHERRY-MAY *is a blowzy, cheerful middle-aged blonde.* FABRICE *is excessively handsome and looks like an advertisement in a health magazine.*)

CHERRY-MAY. (*To* SEBASTIEN.) Is Mr. Jacob Friedland here?

SEBASTIEN. No, madame.

CHERRY-MAY. They said at his office that he would be.

SEBASTIEN. Have you an appointment with him?

CHERRY-MAY. No, but I must see him. It's terribly important. I'm Cherry-May Waterton. Who are you?

SEBASTIEN. My name is Sébastien. I was the late Mr. Sorodin's valet.

CHERRY-MAY. This is Fabrice. (*He bows.*) He doesn't say much but he's sweet when you get to know him, and he doesn't miss a trick.

SEBASTIEN. I'm so relieved.

CHERRY-MAY. (*Looking around.*) Fancy dear old Paul having a valet and a posh place like this. He did come up in the world, didn't he?

JANE. You knew my father?

CHERRY-MAY. My God—(*crossing to* JANE)—are you Paul's daughter? I'm a bloody fool not to have recognized you at once—(*they shake hands*)—there's a strong likeness. (*To* FABRICE, *in execrable French.*) C'est la fille de dear old Paul. (FABRICE *bows.*) I hope we're not intruding, but it really is important that I see Mr. Friedland. I've got a paper here that will interest him.

JANE. A paper? Oh dear!

SEBASTIEN. Perhaps madame would like to sit down. We are expecting Monsieur Friedland at any moment.

CHERRY-MAY. Thanks. That's very civil of you. Fabrice, il faut que nous nous assayons pour attendre jusqu'au Monsieur Friedland vien d'arriver. We've been jogging along in that god-awful bus since lunch-time yesterday.

JANE. Where have you come from?

CHERRY-MAY. Orville-les-Champs, just the other side of Bordeaux. Fabrice's mother runs a little café-restaurant there. Between you and I she's a bad-tempered old bitch —pardon my French—but she certainly can cook. J'ai dit, Fabrice, que ta mère est une cuisinière miraculeuse. He's the apple of her eye, but she gets him down a bit sometimes. That's why we're here really, I mean I think Mr. Friedland might be willing to help.

SEBASTIEN. In what way?

CHERRY-MAY. Well, Fabrice wants a chicken-farm— imagine! (*She laughs.*) He got a sort of "thing" about chickens while he was doing his military service on account of being a cook's assistant or something. I said a garage would be more lively, or even a café-restaurant like his mother's, but no, it's got to be chickens. He's obstinate as a mule once he's set his heart on anything.

JANE. Have you known him long?

CHERRY-MAY. Four years. Ever since he got out of the army. We first met on the beach as a matter of fact. He's a gorgeous swimmer. The moment I clapped eyes on him I said, "Oh dear!" and then when I saw him do that long slow crawl, I said, "Cherry-May, you've had it!" J'ai dit, "Fabrice, que vous nagez comme un poisson." (FABRICE *shrugs his shoulders.*)

SEBASTIEN. This paper, you have it with you?

CHERRY-MAY. Oh yes—it's in my bag. Only a copy of course, the original is in Barclays Bank, St. Jean de Luz.

JANE. You knew my father well?

CHERRY-MAY. You bet I did. I was potty about him for nearly seven years. That's why I left the Jackson Girls.

JANE. Jackson Girls?

CHERRY-MAY. Yes, we were working here at the Casino de Paris, as a matter of fact they're still at it, not the same ones natch, all my lot must have fallen apart years ago.

JANE. When did you first meet him, my father?

CHERRY-MAY. Let's see now. (*She pauses.*) It was March or February, 1930, yes, it must have been March because I was sharing that flat in the rue Washington with Elsie Williams, she was a hot number if ever I saw one, men, nothing but men morning, noon and night. I used to call the joint the Travellers' Club.

JANE. My father was in love with you?

CHERRY-MAY. Oh yes, I think so, for a little while at least. Anyway, I let him persuade me to go racketing off to Shanghai with him. More fool me—I didn't know what I was in for.

SEBASTIEN. How do you mean?

CHERRY-MAY. Oh, I'd rather not go on about all that just now. I mean seeing that this young lady is his daughter, well, it wouldn't be quite the thing, would it?

JANE. You needn't worry about sparing my feelings, Miss Waterton. I haven't seen my father since I was three years old. You say you went to Shanghai with him?

CHERRY-MAY. Oh yes, we had a high old time—that is at first.

JANE. And afterwards?

CHERRY-MAY. Now look here, you and me are friends, aren't we?

JANE. (*With a smile.*) I hope so.

CHERRY-MAY. And I wouldn't want to say anything or do anything to upset you. Your father was a very funny man with very funny ideas. We had a good time together taken by and large, and it was my fault we parted, not his. I just couldn't stand the wear and tear.

JANE. You mean he made you paint pictures?

CHERRY-MAY. Oh, my God! So you know?

JANE. I guessed. That's what the paper's about, isn't it?

CHERRY-MAY. The paper doesn't concern you, dear, that's Mr. Friedland's look-out.

JANE. Had you ever painted before?

CHERRY-MAY. Of course not, and I could only paint then when I had had a few drinks. Paul used to say that alcohol released my dormant genius, that was the phrase he used, I'll never forget it. Finally he made me drink so much that I got jaundice. Ever had jaundice?

JANE. No.

CHERRY-MAY. It's awful! Everything happens in technicolour.

JANE. When did you part?

CHERRY-MAY. August 1939, just before the war.

SEBASTIEN. Where?

CHERRY-MAY. Cairo. We had one of those scenes. Oh dear! He certainly could create all right when he got going. You've never heard such a noise, screaming and roaring and throwing things about! I'm not blaming him, mind you. He treated me very fair. That is, when he calmed down.

SEBASTIEN. You signed the paper in Cairo?

CHERRY-MAY. No, Port Said. It was witnessed by an Arab conjurer and a gentleman from the Lebanon.

SEBASTIEN. Did they read it?

CHERRY-MAY. Oh, no, they couldn't read English. The conjurer had a bit of fun with it, though. He turned it into an egg and then into a rabbit—I must say I couldn't help laughing, but poor old Paul was fit to be tied.

SEBASTIEN. I rather see his point.

CHERRY-MAY. Je vais expliquer cette histoire du papier secret et le lapin, tu le souviens? (FABRICE *gives a sudden loud guffaw, and relapses into silence.*) That story always makes him laugh, he's got a wonderful sense of humour underneath, but he's a bit moody today. I expect it's the bus ride.

SEBASTIEN. It could be almost anything. Did Mr. Sorodin pay you a lump sum down or give you an annuity?

CHERRY-MAY. Just you ask no questions, sonny-boy, and you'll hear no lies. That's Mr. Friedland's business. I've said too much already.

JANE. Anyhow, you parted good friends?

CHERRY-MAY. Oh yes. He packed me on to a P. and O. and that was that. We said good-bye on the promenade deck, we could hardly hear ourselves speak on account of those bloody bugles, but I could see he was upset. I was too. I cried all through lunch.

(*There is the SOUND of VOICES in the hall.* MARIE-CELESTE *opens the door and* ISOBEL *and* PAMELA *enter.* COLIN *and* JACOB *follow.* CHERRY-MAY, JANE *and* FABRICE *rise.*)

ISOBEL. There you are, Jane! I couldn't think what had happened to you. (*She sees* CHERRY-MAY.) Oh!

JANE. (*Crossing to* ISOBEL.) This is Miss Cherry-May Waterton, mother—(ISOBEL *takes a step forward*)—she was a great friend of father's. (ISOBEL *takes a step back.*)

ISOBEL. (*Guardedly.*) How do you do?

JANE. And this is her—her protégé—Monsieur— (*She turns to* CHERRY-MAY *questioningly.*)

CHERRY-MAY. Just call him Fabrice, dear, he hates formality. (*To* FABRICE.) Voici Madame Sorodin, la veuve de tu sais qui. Dis bon jour gentiment. (FABRICE *advances, kisses* ISOBEL'S *hand, then* PAMELA'S *hand. Shakes* JACOB'S *hand then* COLIN'S.)

SEBASTIEN. Miss Waterton wishes to see you on urgent business, Mr. Friedland. It concerns, I suspect, Mr. Sorodin's "Circular" period.

JACOB. (*Sharply.*) What?

SEBASTIEN. She has with her a document.

JACOB. What sort of document?

SEBASTIEN. The usual sort.

CHERRY-MAY. (*To* SEBASTIEN.) Now listen, sonny-boy, you just leave this to me. It's a private matter.

COLIN. (*In a business-like tone.*) If it concerns my late father, it concerns all of us.

CHERRY-MAY. That is for Mr. Friedland to decide after he's read it.

JACOB. (*Crossing to* CHERRY-MAY.) Give it to me, please.

CHERRY-MAY. (*Rising.*) Not here, if it's all the same to you. As I said before, it's a private matter—and it's going to be discussed privately or not at all.

COLIN. (*Pompously.*) We wish to see that paper here and now, so please hand it over without further argument.

CHERRY-MAY. Well, well—look who's talking! A chip off the old block and no mistake—must have his own way when he wants it and where he wants it double-quick pronto! I've got news for you, young man. I didn't come all this way to be brow-beaten, and you can put that where the monkey puts the nuts.

COLIN. We know it's blackmail and we have no time to waste.

CHERRY-MAY. Oh! Using nasty words now, are we? We'll be throwing the furniture about in a minute if I know the form. Come on, Fabrice—we don't want to get ourselves into a free-for-all. (*She makes a movement to go, but* COLIN *bars her way.*)

COLIN. You are not leaving this house until we have seen that document.

ISOBEL. Colin dear, there is no necessity to raise your voice. If this Miss—Miss—er Cherry wishes to discuss the matter privately with Jacob, I think she should be allowed to do so.

PAMELA. I think Colin's perfectly right. The paper concerns us all.

CHERRY-MAY. (*To* PAMELA.) Oh—and who do you think you are when you're at home?

JANE. This is my brother's wife, Miss Waterton.

CHERRY-MAY. I see. Well, I've got a hot flash for her too. (*To* PAMELA.) You stay out of this, dear, unless you want trouble, bad trouble.

PAMELA. (*Grandly.*) Really, Miss Whatever-your-name-is, I am not accustomed to being spoken to in that tone.

CHERRY-MAY. The name is Waterton, Cherry-May Waterton, and now you know, so you can shut up, can't you?

PAMELA. (*Rising.*) How dare you!

CHERRY-MAY. I don't care who you are or what you're accustomed to. I'm just warning you, see? And I'd like to call your high and mighty attention to my young friend over by the window. Just take a good look at those shoulders, dear, and if you don't want to see that pompous, fat-headed husband of yours laid out flat as a pancake you'll keep a civil tongue in your head. Viens, Fabrice—je m'enmerde de tous ces gens. On part.

COLIN. I'm not afraid of your damned gigolo!

ISOBEL. Colin—for heaven's sake . . .

JANE. Be quiet, Colin. You're behaving like an idiot!

CHERRY-MAY. (*Poking* COLIN *with her parasol.*) Stand away from that door, you silly great lout.

COLIN. (*To her.*) I've already told you that you are not going to leave this room before we have seen that document.

CHERRY-MAY. Oh—we'll see about that! (*She goes up to* COLIN *and slaps his face.*) Fabrice! Continuez le bon travail!

JANE. Oh dear, this is most unfortunate—

(*With a loud snarl of rage* FABRICE *hurls himself across*

the room, and fells COLIN *to the ground.* ISOBEL *screams. There is general pandemonium. In the middle of it* MARIE-CELESTE *enters.*)

MARIE-CELESTE. (*Announcing.*) Monsieur Obadiah Lewellyn. (*A respectably dressed but very black NEGRO enters. He is holding a document in his hand.*)
SEBASTIEN. My God! The Jamaican Period!

CURTAIN

ACT THREE

Scene 1

The time is a few hours later.

When the CURTAIN rises there is, as there was in Act Two, Scene 1, an atmosphere of general dejection. ISOBEL *is lying on the sofa with her feet up and her eyes closed.* COLIN, *whose forehead is adorned with a large cross of sticking plaster, is seated Upstage with a plate of food.* PAMELA *and* JANE *are also eating.* JACOB *is sitting in armchair holding* CHERRY-MAY'S *hat.*

JANE. I really think you ought to try to eat something, mother—you've had nothing since lunch and you only just picked at that egg thing.

ISOBEL. (*Hopelessly, with her eyes closed.*) It had garlic in it.

JANE. Shall I ask Marie-Céleste to make you a nice plain omelette?

ISOBEL. No, thank you, dear, I couldn't touch it.

JANE. If you don't eat you'll start one of your headaches.

ISOBEL. I've started one already.

COLIN. Why do you keep on badgering people to eat when they don't want to?

JANE. Well, you didn't need any badgering anyway, you've been stuffing yourself for the last hour.

PAMELA. Why can't we all go back to the hotel?

JANE. Because we can't leave until we know what's happening in there.

PAMELA. (*Glancing towards the library.*) They've been at it for ages.

JANE. Oh, I wish I knew what was going on. (*She goes*

over to the library door and listens.) Sébastien's still talking.

COLIN. In any particular language or just plain English?

PAMELA. (*Giggling.*) Oh, Colin, you do make me laugh, really you do.

JANE. Well, he doesn't make me laugh. If it hadn't been for his oafish, monumental lack of consideration for other people's feelings, he wouldn't have got into that humiliating brawl with the Frenchman and been knocked out.

COLIN. I was not knocked out. I hit my head against the leg of the chair.

JANE. Nonsense. You went down like a ninepin.

COLIN. He took me by surprise.

JANE. The only surprise to me was that he didn't sock you before. You were overbearing and rude and quite insufferable to that poor woman.

PAMELA. I thought she was a horror.

JANE. And she thought you were a pretentious ass, so you were quits, weren't you?

PAMELA. (*Angrily.*) Jane!

COLIN. Poor woman, indeed. She was nothing but a common tart, and the man was quite obviously a pimp.

ISOBEL. Once and for all, Colin, I will not have you using those expressions in my presence. This isn't a barrack-room.

COLIN. I wish to God it was.

ISOBEL. I don't like blasphemy either. I am afraid the army has coarsened you dreadfully, you used to be so well-mannered and gentle when you were a little boy.

JANE. That's what *you* think, mother.

ISOBEL. And now you seem to be growing more and more like your Uncle Edward every day.

PAMELA. (*Hotly.*) It's not fair of you to say that! Colin isn't in the least like Uncle Edward, and, anyway, Uncle Edward would never have been cashiered if it hadn't been for that Mrs. Falkener.

JANE. I don't really feel that we need argue about

Uncle Edward and Mrs. Falkener at the moment, Pamela. We have rather more important matters to discuss.

ISOBEL. I never knew what he saw in her.

JANE. The fact remains that if Colin had not started throwing his weight about and insulting Cherry-May Waterton we shouldn't have had that appalling scene and she and her young man wouldn't have rushed out of the house leaving us with no possible means of tracing them.

PAMELA. I for one don't see any necessity for tracing them, let them both go and a good job.

JACOB. I should have thought, Pamela, that by now even you would have dimly understood that it is vitally important for us to get that document from her and destroy it.

COLIN. And give her an income for life, I suppose. There won't be any estate left at this rate.

JANE. She only wanted a chicken farm.

PAMELA. A chicken farm? What on earth would a woman of that type do with a chicken farm?

JANE. It's for her young man anyhow, she wants to set him up in life. She was perfectly frank and honest about it, and rather touching really, until Colin started bullying her and calling her a blackmailer. Actually she's a very good sort.

COLIN. Good sort! You're dotty.

JANE. She ran away with father years ago because she loved him. She was one of the Jackson Girls.

ISOBEL. Oh no, she wasn't, dear. I knew all three of them when they were young. Veronica, the eldest, came out at the same time as your Aunt Freda. I don't think the other two ever came out at all on account of the war.

JANE. (SEBASTIEN *enters from library and she goes to him.*) Oh, Sébastien—what's happened?

SEBASTIEN. Very little, Miss Jane. I coaxed and cajoled but to no avail.

JACOB. You should have let me handle him.

SEBASTIEN. I fear that even your overwhelming persuasiveness would not have achieved any better results, monsieur.

JACOB. Have you got the paper?
SEBASTIEN. Alas no. I have not.
JANE. Have you read it?
SEBASTIEN. Yes. It's more or less the same as the others.
COLIN. How much did you offer him?
SEBASTIEN. He is not interested in money. He is an Eleventh Hour Immersionist.
ISOBEL. What on earth is that?
SEBASTIEN. An obscure but fairly militant religious sect peculiar to the island of Jamaica, madame.
ISOBEL. Just fancy! One lives and learns, doesn't one?
SEBASTIEN. That is certainly one of the more prevalent human delusions, madame.
ISOBEL. What do—er—Eleventh Hour Immersionists *do* exactly?
SEBASTIEN. I'm not quite clear as to their exact ritual, but I believe they come down from the hills twice a year and dunk themselves in the sea eleven times to the accompaniment of raw-hide drums and some rather dubious wind instruments.
ISOBEL. Oh!
SEBASTIEN. Their dogma is based upon the "It's later than you think" theory.
ISOBEL. I really must tell Father Flanagan, he'll be fascinated . . .
JACOB. (*Patiently.*) Isobel, please. Continue, Sébastien. You say this man is not interested in money?
SEBASTIEN. He is a man of strong religious principles and men of strong religious principles are notoriously uncooperative. Look at Thomas-à-Becket.
ISOBEL. I wouldn't describe Thomas-à-Becket as unco-operative exactly, he was just—
JACOB. Isobel. Thomas-à-Becket's problems were settled several hundred years ago. Our problems are more immediate. Will you please permit us to concentrate on them?
ISOBEL. There's no need to snap at me. 1 really don't know what's happening to everybody today.

COLIN. What did he come here with the paper for if he didn't want to get something out of it?

SEBASTIEN. He intends to publish it.

JANE. Publish it! Oh no!

SEBASTIEN. Oh yes. His conscience has been troubling him for a long long time, and when he read in the Jamaican Daily Gleaner of Sorodin's death, the news so shattered him that he ran out naked into a banana plantation and had a vision.

ISOBEL. What sort of vision?

SEBASTIEN. A vision of your late husband, madame, roasting in hell.

ISOBEL. Good gracious!

SEBASTIEN. His description of it was graphic in the extreme. I will spare you the details but it obviously upset him very much.

ISOBEL. Poor man, it must have.

SEBASTIEN. So much so indeed that he caught the next plane available and came here.

COLIN. But why?

SEBASTIEN. He wishes to save your father's soul, monsieur.

COLIN. He's left it a bit late, hasn't he?

SEBASTIEN. He considers that he was to blame in the first place for having allowed himself to be coerced into painting the pictures.

JACOB. He really did paint them?

SEBASTIEN. Oh yes, every one. He was responsible for the entire Jamaican period.

JACOB. (*Brokenly.*) What have I done—what have I ever done to deserve this?

SEBASTIEN. His personal favourite is "Copra Factory at Sunset"—the one that is at present in the Royal Gallery in Copenhagen.

ISOBEL. Is copra that stuff they get from sea-gulls?

SEBASTIEN. No, madame. Copra is produced by the coco-palm.

ISOBEL. I must be thinking of guano.

JACOB. I implore you, Isobel, in this moment of crisis, to turn your thoughts away from guano.

SEBASTIEN. Mr. Lewellyn is firmly convinced that Mr. Sorodin's soul, in which I think he takes an exaggerated interest, will never achieve proper celestial recognition until that deception is exposed.

COLIN. The poor chap's obviously a religious maniac.

SEBASTIEN. Possibly. At any rate he is quite unshakable.

COLIN. What's he doing now?

SEBASTIEN. Praying for guidance. He may start singing at any moment.

COLIN. I hope to God he doesn't.

ISOBEL. Some negroes have lovely voices.

JACOB. He refused absolutely to take money?

SEBASTIEN. Absolutely.

JACOB. The document is a copy, I presume?

SEBASTIEN. As a matter of fact it isn't. He left a copy in the Bank of Nova Scotia, Port Maria, Jamaica.

JACOB. You mean you actually had it in your hands?

SEBASTIEN. No. He was very cunning. He only let me have a quick glance at it to identify the handwriting, then he made me stand at the other side of the room while he read it aloud to me. I did note, however, that he kept it in his wallet which is something gained at any rate.

JANE. What do you mean, Sébastien?

SEBASTIEN. I mean that it might be possible to extract it if all else fails. I have a friend here in Paris who is an adept at that sort of thing.

JANE. That's quite out of the question, Sébastien.

SEBASTIEN. (*With a shrug.*) Needs must when the devil drives.

JACOB. You say this friend of yours is here in Paris?

JANE. Jacob!

SEBASTIEN. Yes, monsieur. He was a great chum of Mr. Sorodin's. They used to go to race meetings together.

COLIN. A common pickpocket?

SEBASTIEN. Oh no, sir. He only does it as a hobby. He

is actually a pianist by profession. He says it keeps his fingers supple.

COLIN. I must say I didn't expect to come to Paris and get caught up with the underworld.

SEBASTIEN. I always understood that that was the average Englishman's main object in coming to Paris.

COLIN. Was he another of your brother prisoners in the Belgian Congo?

SEBASTIEN. No, sir, in Johannesburg. (*The FRONT DOOR BELL rings.*) Excuse me, sir. (*He goes out.*)

COLIN. That man's utterly without shame.

JANE. I envy him.

(CHERRY-MAY *and* FABRICE *enter, followed by* SEBASTIEN, *who stands by the door.* JACOB *rises.*)

CHERRY-MAY. (*To* JACOB.) I had to come back because I couldn't bear to let the sun go down on my wrath. Besides I left my bloody hat behind. (*Taking hat.*) Ta dear! I lost my temper and it's no use pretending I didn't. (*To* COLIN.) I hope you will accept my apology in the spirit in which it is offered?

COLIN. (*Acutely embarrassed.*) Oh—er—that's perfectly all right.

CHERRY-MAY. (*Noticing the sticking-plaster and going to him.*) Oh, your poor head! Fabrice, regarde ce que tu as fait! Le pauvre garçon est gravement blessé, tu ne sais pas la force de toi-même! Will you accept Fabrice's apology too?

COLIN. Please don't say any more about it.

CHERRY-MAY. Would you mind if he shook hands with you? He won't be happy till he does. He's been in a terrible state all through dinner, wouldn't touch a morsel. He's very neurotic you know, in spite of being so muscular (*she gives a sigh of joy*) and you can take my word for it he won't sleep a wink tonight unless he knows that all's forgiven and forgotten.

COLIN. I still think he might have given me a little warning before hurling himself at me like a thunderbolt.

CHERRY-MAY. Oh, come on, be a sport! It was all my fault really, for flaring up and giving you that slap. I've always been quick off the handle ever since I was a kiddie.

JANE. Be gracious, Colin, it was all a misunderstanding.

COLIN. All right—all right—let's forget it. (*He holds out his hand.*)

CHERRY-MAY. Viens serrer la main avec chaleur, Fabrice. (FABRICE *rushes at* COLIN *and shakes his hand with enthusiasm.*) There. (*Sitting in armchair.*) Now we're all friends again, aren't we?

SEBASTIEN. I am sure that this most heartwarming "amende honorable" calls for some refreshment. Can I offer you a drink, Miss Waterton?

CHERRY-MAY. Thanks. I don't mind if I do.

SEBASTIEN. Champagne?

CHERRY-MAY. Oh no, champagne gives me the come-ups. A whiskey splash if it's not too much trouble, and some ginger ale for Fabrice on account of he's in training.

SEBASTIEN. In training? (*He looks at* FABRICE, *then turns to* CHERRY-MAY *with a knowing smile.*) I quite understand.

CHERRY-MAY. (*To* FABRICE.) Tout va s'arranger, chéri, c'est inutile d'avoir l'air d'un canard mourant dans un orage de tonnerre. (FABRICE *grunts morosely.* CHERRY-MAY, *in order to get* ISOBEL'S *attention, hits* ISOBEL'S *knee with her umbrella.* ISOBEL'S *leg, responding to the reflex action, shoots into the air.*) You mustn't think he's sulky, it's just that he shuts up like a clam when he's upset. I hope you're enjoying your stay in Paris, Mrs. Sorodin?

ISOBEL. (*Taken by surprise.*) Well, I—er—I'm afraid that in the present circumstances—

CHERRY-MAY. (*Realising her blunder.*) Oh dear—there I go again—putting my foot into it up to the neck. I ought to have my head examined.

JACOB. (*With studied irony.*) Without wishing to disrupt this rather convulsive flow of social amenities, Miss

Waterton, I think it would be a good idea to return to the business in hand.

CHERRY-MAY. You mean the paper?

JACOB. Yes. Have you got it?

CHERRY-MAY. Yes, here in my bag—but . . .

JACOB. I fully understand your reluctance to discuss so private a matter in the presence of Paul Sorodin's family . . .

CHERRY-MAY. I don't wish to seem carping, dear, but if only you'd said that before we'd all have been saved a lot of fuss and fume.

SEBASTIEN. Your whiskey splash, Miss Waterton.

CHERRY-MAY. (*Taking it.*) Ta. (SEBASTIEN *hands* FABRICE *a ginger ale.*)

JACOB. I understand from Miss Jane Sorodin that you wish to invest in a small chicken farm.

CHERRY-MAY. I didn't say anything about it being small.

JACOB. Well, assuming that everything else is satisfactorily arranged I really feel that the exact acreage can be discussed later.

CHERRY-MAY. It isn't for me, anyway. Personally I can't bear the bloody things—pardon my French, Mrs. Sorodin.

ISOBEL. (*Determined to be amiable.*) I fear my own French is sadly inadequate. I always regretted that my parents didn't send me to a convent when I was a child. My sister Freda on the other hand speaks it like a native. When she was seventeen she was sent to Geneva to be finished.

CHERRY-MAY. I should think Geneva'd be enough to finish anybody.

JACOB. (*With commendable restraint.*) Although at any other time I should be the first to welcome an intelligent discussion of the League of Nations.

COLIN. (*Cheerfully.*) We've almost formed one ourselves now, anyhow, haven't we?

PAMELA. (*Giggling.*) Oh, Colin—how can you?

JACOB. God give me strength!

ISOBEL. Jacob, please!

JACOB. That was not intended as blasphemy, Isobel. It was a last despairing cry from a tormented man who is being driven step by step into a nervous collapse.

JANE. Keep calm, Jacob. You really mustn't work yourself into another state. You'll have a stroke!

JACOB. (*Wildly.*) I should welcome it!

ISOBEL. You shouldn't say things like that, Jacob, even in fun.

JACOB. I did not say it in fun, Isobel. (FABRICE *leans over* JACOB, *watching him.*) The dreadful happenings of the last few days have banished for ever the word "fun" from my personal vocabulary. (JACOB *turns and sees* FABRICE.) Go away. I have tried to keep my head in this appalling situation. I have struggled, against overwhelming odds, to deal sanely and practically with the problems that beset us, for your sake, Isobel, as well as for my own, and have I received the slightest co-operation? The answer is no! A thousand times NO! Your lack of concentration both individually and as a family verges on the pathological. Your unlimited capacity for irrelevant reminiscence has beaten me to the dust. During these pregnant hours which so vitally affect the lives of all of us I have been regaled by descriptions of your sister Freda and her linguistic abilities, the mystic attributes of your Father Confessor, the misdemeanours of your brother Edward with a Mrs.—Mrs.—

EVERYONE. (*But* CHERRY-MAY *and* FABRICE *say this together.*) Falkener.

JACOB. And when Sébastien emerged from the library a little while ago, you, Isabel, were engrossed in the social frustrations of the Jackson Girls.

CHERRY-MAY. What's the matter with the Jackson Girls?

COLIN. One of them came out and the other two didn't.

CHERRY-MAY. I'll bet that was Elsie Williams. She was always a pusher. Out of what?

JACOB. I give up. I am defeated. I can do no more and say no more. I am a broken man.

JANE. Give Mr. Friedland a whiskey and soda, Sébastien.

SEBASTIEN. Certainly, Miss Jane. (*He goes to the table and mixes a drink.*)

ISOBEL. I'm sure I don't know what *I've* done that Jacob should attack me in that hysterical manner.

JANE. Never mind, darling, he's having a very trying time.

COLIN. So are we. (SEBASTIEN *hands* JACOB *his drink.*)

PAMELA. If you ask me, I think he was very rude indeed. Why shouldn't mother talk about Aunt Freda and the Jackson Girls as much as she wants to?

CHERRY-MAY. Here, what *is* all this about the Jackson Girls? Who's been saying what? I can tell you one thing, their dance routines were just as good as the Tillers' any day of the week!

JANE. It's a slight misunderstanding, Miss Waterton.

CHERRY-MAY. (*Still a trifle suspicious.*) Oh.

SEBASTIEN. With regard to that chicken farm, Miss Waterton—

CHERRY-MAY. What about it?

SEBASTIEN. If Mr. Friedland made you a satisfactory offer, would you be willing to hand over the paper that Mr. Sorodin made you sign?

CHERRY-MAY. I might be willing to consider it.

SEBASTIEN. And would you also agree to sign another paper with Mr. Friedland and his lawyer guaranteeing to keep the whole matter entirely secret?

CHERRY-MAY. (*After a slight pause.*) Yes—that is—if, as you say, the offer Mr. Friedland makes me is satisfactory.

SEBASTIEN. Good.

CHERRY-MAY. But the paper's in St. Jean de Luz, you know, the real one.

SEBASTIEN. In that case, after your conversation with Mr. Friedland in his office tomorrow morning, would you and Monsieur Fabrice be willing to go to Biarritz, collect the document, and fly back here with it within twenty-four hours?

CHERRY-MAY. Well, I don't know about that—flying gives me the willies.

SEBASTIEN. Perhaps, if your expenses were—er—handsomely defrayed, you might be able to bring yourself to endure the willies?

CHERRY-MAY. All right. Anything would be better than that smelly bus.

SEBASTIEN. You know where Mr. Friedland's office is?

CHERRY-MAY. Yes, we went there this morning.

SEBASTIEN. Would ten o'clock tomorrow be convenient to you, Mr. Friedland?

JACOB. If I am not in a strait-jacket, yes.

(*There is the sound of a deep negro VOICE in the library singing "Let us Break Bread Together on Our Knees."*)

CHERRY-MAE. My God, what's that?

ISOBEL. (*Rising to the occasion.*) A friend of ours from the West Indies.

CHERRY-MAY. Écoute, chéri—c'est une jolie voix, n'est-ce pas? (*To the room in general.*) He's potty about music. (*She rises.*) Il faut que nous partions maintenant, nous ne voulons pas dépasser notre bienvenue.

JANE. (*Holding out her hand and rising.*) Good-bye, Miss Waterton. I do hope we shall meet again some day. (JACOB *rises.* SEBASTIEN *opens the double doors.*)

CHERRY-MAY. So do I, dear. You must come to see us at our chicken farm, we'll give you a nice new-laid egg. (*The song changes to "My Lord, What a Morning." To* ISOBEL.) Good-bye, Mrs. Sorodin, it's been a pleasure, I'm sure. Good-bye, Mr. Friedland. See you in the morning. Fabrice, viens dire bonsoir à Madame Sorodin.

(FABRICE *rushes at* ISOBEL, *who shrinks slightly. He kisses her hand and then goes to shake hands with* JACOB *when* OBADIAH, *still singing, enters from the library.* FABRICE *shakes his hand.* OBADIAH *shrugs his shoulders and, still singing, goes back into the library.*)

JANE. (*Helplessly.*) Oh dear!

CHERRY-MAY. He'll have the plaster off the ceiling if he's not careful. (*She listens.*) I once knew a man in Belfast with a voice just like that, his name was Flanagan. Bye-bye, all. (*Goes out with* FABRICE.)

JACOB. There must be just one person in Ireland called O'Reilly.

(*SONG changes to "Every Time I Feel a Spirit."*)

ISOBEL. (*Rising.*) I really can't stand this any longer— this noise is going through my head like a knife.

COLIN. All right, mother, Pam and I will take you to the hotel.

JANE. What are we to do about Mr. Lewellyn, Jacob? What are we to do?

SEBASTIEN. Leave it all to me, Miss Jane.

JANE. Oh dear— I don't like it— I really don't.

COLIN. Come on, Jane. (*The singing stops.*) Mother's exhausted.

JACOB. Go with your mother, dear. I'll deal with this.

JANE. All right.

ISOBEL. (*At the door, stiffly.*) Good-night, Jacob. (JANE *goes.*) I hope that you will feel better in the morning. (*Sweeps out, followed by* COLIN *and* PAMELA.)

SEBASTIEN. You'd better go too, sir. You need a good night's rest.

JACOB. What are you going to do?

SEBASTIEN. Leave it all to me. I'll handle it with the utmost dispatch. You're in a highly excitable state. I suggest a glass of hot milk, two tablets of Nebutol— they're twilight sleep but don't let that discourage you. (*He leads* JACOB *out.*)

JACOB. All right. Thank you, Sébastien. I am most grateful.

SEBASTIEN. De rien, Monsieur Friedland. Good-night.

NUDE WITH VIOLIN

JACOB. (*As he goes out.*) Good-night. (SEBASTIEN *closes the doors. The VOICE in the library continues humming "Swing Low Sweet Chariot."* SEBASTIEN *comes quickly back, goes to the telephone.*)

SEBASTIEN. (*At telephone.*) Clichy 5657?—Allô—Ici Sébastien. Oui, très bien—Joe est là? Bon—J'attends. (*A slight pause.*) Allô, Joe? This is Bass. Pop round here there's a good boy, there's a bit of trouble on and I need your help—no, no knives or firearms necessary, it's just a question of finesse—you might slip a cosh into your pocket in case things get a bit dodgy. Are all the boys in the bar? Well round 'em all up. Tell dear old Paul to bring his hypodermic—you never know. Five minutes time? Okey dokey—Abyssinia. (*He hangs up the receiver, takes off his coat, and starts for the library, rolling up his sleeves as he goes.*)

THE CURTAIN FALLS

ACT THREE

SCENE 2

The time is about eleven a.m. on the following morning.

In the window on an easel, facing the audience, is a vast canvas. Standing before this, with an ecstatic expression on his face, is CLINTON PREMINGER, *junior. Down Right is* GEORGE, *a press photographer with a camera and flash bulbs.* SEBASTIEN *is sitting negligently on the arm of the sofa, smoking a cigarette.*

CLINTON. This is the greatest moment of my life.
SEBASTIEN. I'm so glad.
CLINTON. Get one from this angle, George—sort of oblique.
GEORGE. Okay. (*He takes a flash picture.*)

SEBASTIEN. (*Glancing at his watch.*) Time's up. They'll be here in a minute.

CLINTON. One more, please, one more.

SEBASTIEN. Very well but hurry up.

CLINTON. I want you in this one, just gazing with a rapt expression.

SEBASTIEN. Certainly not.

CLINTON. Come on, be a pal. *Life* Magazine will just eat it.

SEBASTIEN. If I could be sure of that I might oblige.

CLINTON. Please, just one, the personal touch means so much.

SEBASTIEN. Who to?

CLINTON. The whole of the United States.

SEBASTIEN. In that case I dare not refuse. (*He crushes out his cigarette.*) Where do you want me to stand?

CLINTON. (*Indicating.*) About here. Is that okay for you, George?

GEORGE. (*Laconically.*) I'm beyond caring.

SEBASTIEN. Aren't you interested in photographing modern paintings?

GEORGE. No sir. Not when they look like that.

CLINTON. If you saw that picture for the first time, what would you say?

GEORGE. I'd say, boy is that dame in trouble.

CLINTON. It's a great masterpiece.

GEORGE. Okay, okay, it's a great masterpiece. I'm not arguing, let's shoot.

SEBASTIEN. The latest offer for it, from one of your own countrymen, was eighty thousand dollars.

GEORGE. Don't think I'm boasting, mister, but we got suckers in America the same as anywhere else. Turn your head a bit to the left—ready— (*He flashes.*) Okay.

SEBASTIEN. My mouth was open.

GEORGE. So was mine. (*To* CLINTON.) Finito?

CLINTON. Yes. That's all—rush them through.

GEORGE. I can't wait. (*He goes out.*)

SEBASTIEN. A rugged character.

CLINTON. (*Depressed.*) I can't bear it—I just can't bear it.
SEBASTIEN. What?
CLINTON. This God-damned philistinism, this dumb, ignorant hostility to anything that's progressive in Art—When you think of what Sorodin has done for the world, and then a jerk like that comes along and sneers, it's heartbreaking.
SEBASTIEN. Cheer up. The avant-garde is always in a vulnerable position. You must steel yourself against the slings and arrows of the multitude.
CLINTON. He photographed that picture, he looked at it from every angle, but never for one moment did he really see it. He never even noticed the brushwork.
SEBASTIEN. You cannot go through life expecting people to notice brushwork.
CLINTON. I know, I know—I guess I mind too much. After all it's been the same all through the history of Art, hasn't it? Do you ever think of Wagner?
SEBASTIEN. Constantly.

(*At this moment* ISOBEL, JANE, PAMELA, *and* COLIN *enter.*)

ISOBEL. Good morning, Sébastien.
SEBASTIEN. Good morning, madame. (*They shake hands.*)
ISOBEL. Where is Mr. Friedland? He told us to meet him here.
SEBASTIEN. I am expecting him at any moment, madame.
ISOBEL. I hope he won't be late—we're catching the one o'clock plane.
CLINTON. (*Crossing to her and shaking her hand.*) Good morning, Mrs. Sorodin. I guess I owe you an apology.
ISOBEL. (*Politely.*) Oh, indeed—what for?
CLINTON. For getting in your hair so much.
ISOBEL. (*Startled.*) Getting in my hair?

CLINTON. I mean always busting in and out and intruding on your sorrow.

ISOBEL. Oh! My sorrow! (*She laughs.*)

CLINTON. But I've seen it now—and photographed it and everything's fine—so I won't trouble you any more. Good-bye, and thanks a lot. (*Goes out quickly.*)

ISOBEL. You know I cannot understand a single word that young man says. Oh dear. (*She catches sight of the picture.*)

COLIN. (*Staring at it.*) Good Lord! Look at this, Pam.

PAMELA. Oh! (*She goes into gales of laughter.*)

JANE. (*She looks at the picture.*) Oh! It can't be true—it really can't. (*She also breaks down and laughs helplessly.*)

COLIN. Is that the one they're coming to see? The one that they're making all the fuss about?

SEBASTIEN. It is, sir.

JANE. Look, mother, you really must look! (*She is in paroxysms of laughter.*)

ISOBEL. No dear—really—I'd rather not—

JANE. I insist. (*Choking with laughter she forces* ISOBEL *to look at the picture.*)

ISOBEL. No, no— I really— Oh! (*She collapses with laughter and chokes.* EVERYONE *but* SEBASTIEN *is now out of control.* JACOB *comes in. His face looks harassed and drawn. He stands at the door for a moment looking at the scene in astonishment.*)

JACOB. What on earth is happening?

ISOBEL. Jacob—I'm sorry—I can't help it—

JANE. (*Gasping.*) It's the picture, Jacob—we've just seen it.

JACOB. Control yourself, Isobel, for heaven's sake! Have you all gone mad?

SEBASTIEN. (*To* JACOB.) Hysteria has set in I'm afraid, monsieur.

JANE. (*Wiping her eyes.*) We'll be all right in a minute, Jacob, just give us a little time.

PAMELA. It's those feet! They're such a funny shape— (*She goes off again.*)

JANE. Do stop. We *must* pull ourselves together.
JACOB. I should like a small brandy and soda please, Sébastien. I am not feeling very well this morning.
SEBASTIEN. (*Going to the table.*) Certainly, monsieur.
JANE. (*Contritely.*) Oh, I am sorry, Jacob.
ISOBEL. The dreadful thing is that it *has* got a distinct look of poor Mrs. Etheridge— Oh— Oh— Oh—! (*She presses her handkerchief to her eyes.*)
JANE. Mother!
ISOBEL. I don't know what I shall do the next time I run into her in Sloane Street—
SEBASTIEN. (*To* JACOB.) Your brandy and soda, monsieur.
JACOB. Thank you. (*Drinks.*)
SEBASTIEN. Lift up your heart, monsieur. I have good news for you. Mr. Obadiah Lewellyn is at this moment on his way back to Jamaica.
JACOB. (*Jumping.*) What?
SEBASTIEN. I tried to telephone you first thing this morning but your line was out of order.
JACOB. The paper. What about the paper?
SEBASTIEN. He tore it up, monsieur.
JACOB. *He* tore it up? What do you mean?
SEBASTIEN. It took rather a long while to get him into the right mood but we ultimately succeeded.
JANE. We?
SEBASTIEN. Before attempting to reason with Mr. Lewellyn I took the precaution of telephoning to a few of my friends. I felt it wise to be prepared for any eventuality.
JANE. You didn't do anything to him, did you, Sébastien?
SEBASTIEN. Oh no, Miss Jane. As a matter of fact the boot was on the other foot.
COLIN. What are you talking about?
SEBASTIEN. Actually it was he who did something to us.
JACOB. What do you mean? What could he do to you?
SEBASTIEN. He saved us, monsieur.

JACOB. Saved you?

SEBASTIEN. Yes. That is we encouraged him to believe that he had.

COLIN. What the hell are you talking about?

SEBASTIEN. When I entered the library, Mr. Lewellyn was not only singing himself into an ecstatic trance, he was also undressing.

ISOBEL. (*Startled.*) Undressing? Whatever for?

SEBASTIEN. A not uncommon Freudian impulse, madame.

ISOBEL. I hope you stopped him.

SEBASTIEN. Oh no, madame. To attempt to frustrate anyone in a state of such spiritual abandon might have lead to the most appalling consequences. All I could do in the circumstances was to fold his garments neatly, as he discarded them, and let him rip.

ISOBEL. Did he take *everything* off?

SEBASTIEN. Everything but his glasses, madame.

ISOBEL. How very surprising! He looked such a mild respectable man. There's no accounting for what people will do nowadays. Do you remember that clergyman in Bletchley?

JACOB. (*Irritably.*) Isobel, please—

JANE. Go on, Sébastien. What happened then?

SEBASTIEN. Oh, from then on everything was easy. When my friends arrived he stopped singing and invited us to join him in prayer.

COLIN. That must have shaken your friends a bit.

SEBASTIEN. Oh no sir, being men of the underworld they naturally took in the situation at a glance. Then Mr. Lewellyn suddenly felt the urge for total immersion, so we moved into the bathroom; and do you know, taken by and large, the service went off very well.

JANE. Service?

SEBASTIEN. Not perhaps according to accepted Caribbean standards, but quite satisfactory within its limits. Then, when we had dried ourselves, Mr. Lewellyn exhorted us to see the light, to which we agreed unanimously, then as a final gesture he destroyed the paper as an act of Faith.

COLIN. Well, I'll be damned.

SEBASTIEN. I took the liberty on your behalf, Mr. Friedland, of promising him a new stained glass window for his church. I told him that the money would be cabled to Jamaica immediately.

JACOB. How much?

SEBASTIEN. His rough estimate amounted to thirty-five pounds seventeen shillings and sixpence. I suggested that fifty pounds would be safer in case of unforeseen extras. You know, a cup of coffee here, cup of cocoa there, it does mount up you know—

JACOB. Thank you, Sébastien. You did very well. I am most grateful.

ISOBEL. I presume he dressed again before going to the airport?

SEBASTIEN. Oh yes, madame. When his ecstasy subsided he became quite normal. He actually complained of the climate being a bit nippy.

JANE. I can see why my father was so fond of you, Sébastien. You are certainly resourceful.

SEBASTIEN. Mademoiselle is most flattering.

JANE. What do we do now?

COLIN. What do you mean?

JANE. The three great periods of my father's painting have been accounted for and disposed of. What about the fourth?

SEBASTIEN. (*Suavely.*) The fourth, Miss Jane?

JACOB. That is precisely what has been keeping me awake all night.

JANE. That monstrosity. (*She points towards the easel.*) Who painted that?

SEBASTIEN. Your directness of approach does you credit, Miss Jane.

JANE. Did you paint it yourself?

SEBASTIEN. I thought that that was in your mind, Miss Jane.

JACOB. Stop beating about the bush, Sébastien. Did you or didn't you?

SEBASTIEN. No, monsieur, I did not.

JACOB. Well, if you didn't who in heaven's name did?

(*One of the double doors opens and* STOTESBURY *runs in.*)

STOTESBURY. (*Crossing to the picture.*) Then it's true!

SEBASTIEN. Stotesbury. Why aren't you at school?

STOTESBURY. How could you do such a cruel, wicked thing? You've broken your promise.

SEBASTIEN. Control yourself, Stotesbury. (*To* ISOBEL.) Forgive this abrupt intrusion, madame. This is my son.

JANE. Your son!

SEBASTIEN. Dis "Bon Jour" gentiment Stotesbury.

STOTESBURY. (*Stamping his foot.*) I won't!

ISOBEL. What a dear little boy. Why is he called Stotesbury?

SEBASTIEN. His mother had ideas above her station.

STOTESBURY. (*Shouting.*) I'll never forgive you—never, never, never!

ISOBEL. Why are you in such a temper, little boy?

STOTESBURY. Because my father is a bastard.

SEBASTIEN. As a matter of fact that is about the only thing we have in common.

ISOBEL. Well, really I—I hardly think— (*She breaks off.*)

SEBASTIEN. Run away now, Stotesbury, like a good boy. I will explain everything later.

STOTESBURY. You promised on your word of honour not to show it to anyone until it was finished.

JACOB. Good God! Do you mean— (*To* STOTESBURY.) Was it you who painted that picture?

STOTESBURY. Of course it was. It's my masterpiece. I had to do quite a lot of it on a ladder.

SEBASTIEN. Now look here, Stotesbury. This picture is my property, finished or unfinished. You have been well paid for it.

STOTESBURY. (*Contemptuously.*) Well paid! Two hundred francs and a box of Carlsbad plums.
SEBASTIEN. *And* a matinée at the Opéra Comique.
STOTESBURY. It was only "The Tales of Hoffmann."
SEBASTIEN. You can't always expect "Norma." Go to your room.
STOTESBURY. But the painting isn't finished. Won't you please let me fix it? The right breast's all wrong.
SEBASTIEN. Both breasts are all wrong. Go away.
STOTESBURY. I'll never paint another picture for you again—never as long as I live. You have no soul. (*He stomps out and slams the door.*)
SEBASTIEN. (*Calling after him.*) Don't you bellow at me. You're a ghastly little toad. (*To the others.*) You know, that boy has already worn out three psychiatrists.
JACOB. Do you mean to tell me that that child painted that picture unaided?
SEBASTIEN. Certainly, sir. He is a diligent boy. As you can see, his draughtsmanship still leaves a little to be desired and his sense of anatomy is a bit erratic, but he's young as yet. It's his maturity that we dread. His other canvasses of course are more abstract.
JACOB. Other canvases?
SEBASTIEN. Yes. About thirty all told. Mr. Sorodin signed them all.
JACOB. This is grotesque!
SEBASTIEN. He described them as his "Neo-Infantilism" period. He dearly loved a good joke. (*He laughs.*)
JACOB. Where are they?
SEBASTIEN. In a warehouse in Passy, monsieur.
COLIN. They must be destroyed immediately.
SEBASTIEN. (*Crossing to* COLIN.) I think not, monsieur. That would be a futile gesture of vandalism. If judiciously placed on the market during the next few years they should fetch anything up to a hundred thousand pounds. I have already insured them for eighty thousand.
JACOB. *You* have insured them?
SEBASTIEN. Yes, monsieur. They are my property. Nat-

urally enough really considering that my son painted them. Mr. Sorodin saw the justice of that which is the reason he assigned them to me to dispose of as I saw fit. He suggested that you and I might come to some sort of arrangement.

JACOB. I'll see you damned first! I'll expose the whole abominable swindle!

SEBASTIEN. (*Suavely.*) Wouldn't that be a little inconsistent seeing that you have already paid off Princess Pavlikov, Miss Waterton and Mr. Lewellyn? I really do advise you to think carefully, Mr. Friedland. If you expose the whole abominable swindle, as you call it, you also expose yourself to the ridicule of the world.

COLIN. (*Rising.*) On behalf of my mother and my family I would like to say that I entirely agree with Mr. Friedland. The scandal must be exposed and we must face the consequences. Don't you agree, mother?

ISOBEL. Yes—I suppose so—but—

COLIN. (*Sitting again.*) But what?

ISOBEL. I was thinking of that dear little boy—after all that work—he'll be dreadfully disappointed.

SEBASTIEN. Not only will *he* be disappointed, the whole world of modern painting will be humiliated and impoverished. The casualties in Hollywood alone will be appalling. The bottom will fall out of the market and thousands of up and coming young artists will starve. It will be a cataclysm! Many of the great masters too will be flung into disrepute, their finest pictures will be viewed with suspicion and distrust. If the news leaks out that the great Sorodin's masterpieces were painted by a Russian tart, an ex-Jackson Girl, an Eleventh Hour Immersionist and a boy of fourteen, the rot will spread like wildfire. Modern sculpture, music, drama and poetry will all shrivel in the holocaust. Think what will happen to those tens of thousands of industrious people who today are earning a comfortable livelihood by writing without grammar, composing without harmony and painting without form. These poor miserable wretches will either be flung into abject poverty or forced really to learn their jobs. Reputations will wither overnight. No one will be spared. Not even Grandma Moses.

ISOBEL. I see no reason to drag in the Old Testament.

SEBASTIEN. Pause and consider, Mr. Friedland, before you unleash this chaos. It will not only be ridicule that you have to fear, it will be crucifixion! Your colleagues alone will see to that. (*The FRONT DOOR BELL rings.*) Here are two of them now.

JANE. What are you going to do, Jacob?

SEBASTIEN. (*To* JACOB.) Is our little secret to be kept inviolate, monsieur, or laid wide open?

JACOB. Come to my office this afternoon. We'll discuss it there.

SEBASTIEN. And Sir Alaric Craigie and Mr. Elmore P. Riskin?

JACOB. (*Despairingly.*) Show them in.

SEBASTIEN. Very good, monsieur. (*He places two chairs in front of the picture, then bows to* ISOBEL, *then to* JACOB, *and opens the double doors.*)

THE CURTAIN FALLS

PROPERTY LIST

General Set Dressing:
  Sofa
  7 side chairs
  Sofa table
  Arm chair
  Desk
  2 commodes
  2 end tables
  Wrought iron table
  2 wrought iron chairs
  Stool
  4 table lamps
  Accessory decoration such as flowers, pictures, books, objets d'art, etc.

WORKING PROPS

ACT ONE

Scene 1

On the Set:
  On Bar Table:
    Silver tray
    2 decanters (filled)
    7 champagne glasses
    Magnum of champagne with large black bow
    Small bottle gingerale
    Bottle opener
    Bar towel
  Cigarette boxes on all tables
  Ash trays on all tables
  Boxes of matches on all tables
  Telephone

PROPERTY PLOT

Off Left:
  Plate of cookies
  Jar of paté on small tray
  Wads of paper (Pocket size—including nude postcard
     and typed "Sorodin" letter) (All for SEBASTIEN)
Up Center:
  Briefcase with papers and pencil (CLINTON)
  Pocket note pad (CLINTON)

ACT TWO

SCENE 1

Set:
  3 plates of food, forks, napkins. (For JANE, COLIN, *and*
     PAMELA)
  On Bar Table:
    Ice bucket with tongs and ice cubes
    6 highball glasses
    2 Manhattan glasses
    Seltzer bottle, full

Strike:
  Used champagne glasses
  Champagne bottle
  Sweep up broken glass

Up Center:
  Cablegram (for CLINTON)
  Typed letter (for ANYA)
  Document for OBADIAH

Off Left:
  Brandy snifter, with Brandy, on tray

PROPERTY PLOT
ACT TWO

Scene 2

Strike:
 Brandy snifter
 All food plates, forks, napkins

ACT THREE

Scene 1

Set:
 3 plates of food, forks, napkins (for JANE, COLIN, and
  PAMELA)

Up Center:
 Sticking plaster for COLIN
 Camera with flash attachment (for GEORGE)

ACT THREE

Scene 2

Set:
 Change furniture to new marks
 Easel and picture of "Nude With Violin"

Strike:
 Used plates, forks, napkins

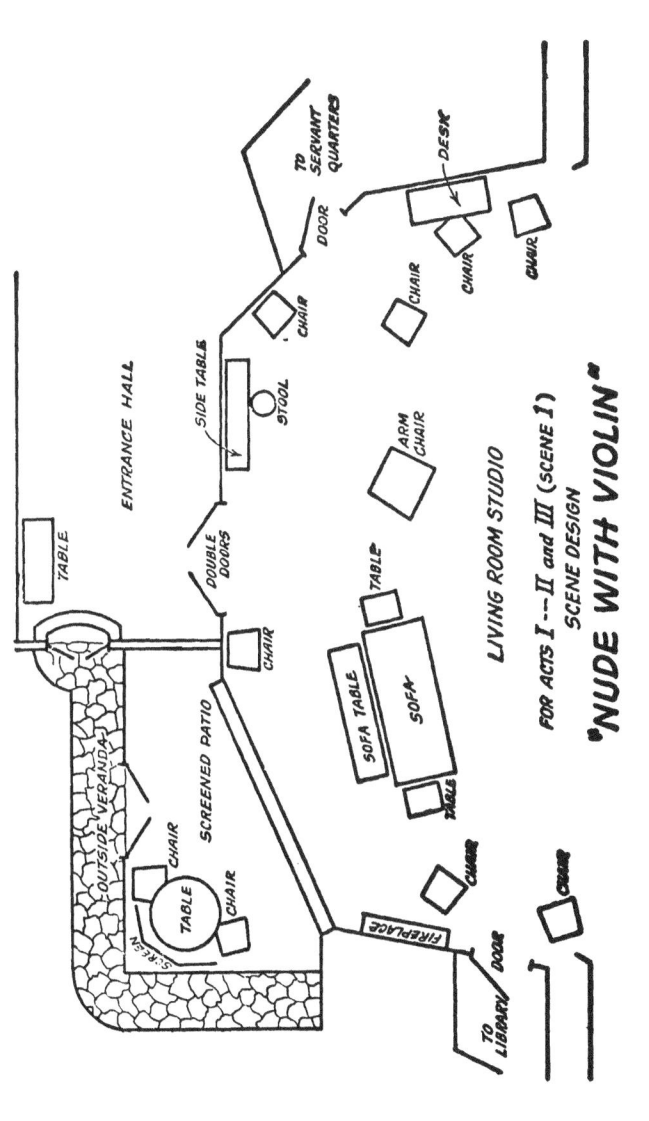

MUSIC USE NOTE

Licensees are solely responsible for obtaining formal written permission from copyright owners to use copyrighted music in the performance of this play and are strongly cautioned to do so. If no such permission is obtained by the licensee, then the licensee must use only original music that the licensee owns and controls. Licensees are solely responsible and liable for all music clearances and shall indemnify the copyright owners of the play(s) and their licensing agent, Samuel French, against any costs, expenses, losses and liabilities arising from the use of music by licensees. Please contact the appropriate music licensing authority in your territory for the rights to any incidental music.

IMPORTANT BILLING AND CREDIT REQUIREMENTS

If you have obtained performance rights to this title, please refer to your licensing agreement for important billing and credit requirements.

www.ingramcontent.com/pod-product-compliance
Lightning Source LLC
Chambersburg PA
CBHW071833290426
44109CB00017B/1814